SUCCESSFUL
ADOPTIVE FAMILIES

SUCCESSFUL ADOPTIVE FAMILIES

A Longitudinal Study of Special Needs Adoption

VICTOR GROZE

Foreword by James A. Rosenthal

Westport, Connecticut
London

Library of Congress Cataloging-in-Publication Data

Groze, Victor K.
   Successful adoptive families : a longitudinal study of special
needs adoption / by Victor Groze ; foreword by James A. Rosenthal.
     p.   cm.
   Includes bibliographical references and index.
   ISBN 0–275–95343–2
   1. Special needs adoption—United States—Longitudinal studies.
I. Title.
HV875.55.G76   1996
362.7′34—dc20   95–11264

British Library Cataloguing in Publication Data is available.

Library of Congress Catalog Card Number: 95–11264
ISBN: 0–275–95343–2

First published in 1996

Praeger Publishers, 88 Post Road West, Westport, CT 06881
An imprint of Greenwood Publishing Group, Inc.

Printed in the United States of America

The paper used in this book complies with the
Permanent Paper Standard issued by the National
Information Standards Organization (Z39.48–1984).

10 9 8 7 6 5 4 3 2 1

Copyright Acknowledgments

The author and the publisher gratefully acknowledge permission to use the following:

Excerpts from Victor Groze, "Clinical and Nonclinical Adoptive Families of Special Needs Children." *Families in Society* 75 (February 1994), 90–104. Published by Families International, Inc.

Excerpts from Victor Groze, "A 1 and 2 Year Follow-up Study of Adoptive Families and Special
Needs Children." In press, *Children and Youth Services Review.*

Excerpts from V. Groze, M. Haines-Simeon, and R. P. Barth, "Barriers in Permanency Planning for
Medically Fragile Children: Drug Affected Children and HIV Infected Children." *Child and Adolescent Social Work Journal* 11 (January 1994), 63–85.

Excerpts from Victor Groze, "Adoption, Attachment and Self-Concept." *Child and Adolescent Social
Work Journal* 9 (February 1992), 169–191.

To

Michial Zane Jennings

and

*the adoptive families who shared
part of their lives with me over 4 years.*

Contents

Tables and Figures

TABLES

FIGURES

Foreword

Special needs adoption has moved through several phases. For many years, older children or children with handicaps or emotional problems have been adopted but only in the past 20 to 25 years has adoption emerged as the preferred option when children with special needs cannot live with their birth families.

As the special needs adoption movement gained momentum in the 1970s, practitioners increasingly recognized that "it worked." Kids with traumatic histories and with serious disabilities were successfully adopted. They made great and unexpected progress. Families derived great joy. The slogan "No child is unadoptable" emerged. As special needs adoption matured, real-world realities intruded. Along with successes came increases in adoption disruptions (terminations of the adoption), painful to both child and family. Practitioners and researchers began to recognize the challenges that children faced in adapting and attaching to new family systems, as well as the difficulties that families had in adapting to the children. As adoption became an option for greater numbers of children, the child welfare system increasingly struggled to find adoptive homes. Many children with special needs, particularly, children of color, are stranded in out-of-home placement while social workers search for adoptive homes.

We recognize now that while the effects of trauma disappear for some, these effects have lasting impact for many others. Many children, even those with no developmental delays, present difficult challenges in behavior, school, and family relationships long after adoptive placement. Dr. Victor Groze's book talks about the real-world strategies that families use to make adoption work. Even if effects of trauma persist, families can develop the resources, skills, and social supports to adapt to, and deal with, these traumas.

Dr. Groze's book brings a much-needed longitudinal perspective to adoption research. One gets a sense of how adoption looks and feels for the sample of families as they move forward across the 4 years that the study encompasses. His work provides support for many of the cross-sectional studies that have been published in the last decade. He focuses in depth on the impacts of physical and sexual abuse and on sibling adoption issues. He provides insight into the nature and function of social support in the family. Results are examined in the context of a family system model that focuses on both strengths and deficits. The study results are informative for researchers and academics; the writing and text are accessible and practical for parents and practitioners.

Successful Adoptive Families help enhance theoretical and practical knowledge and guide policy and practice as special needs adoption moves toward the year 2000.

James A. Rosenthal
Associate Professor
University of Oklahoma School of Social Work
March 12, 1995

Preface

Adoption research represents an integration of the personal with the professional aspects of my life. My interest in adoption began by growing up in a home with an adoptive brother, who was the fourth child to join my sibling group of 5 children. He would have been classified as a special needs child had the term been coined in the 1960s. Life with him had many highs and lows, and it was always interesting.

My interest in adoption was renewed while I was pursuing my doctoral work. In order to supplement my income, I was hired by an adoption agency to conduct home studies of prospective adoptive parents for children with special needs and to provide supervision to the family after a child was placed for adoption. My first 2 cases ended in disruption, that is, the removal of the child from the adoptive home before legalization of the adoption. This difficulty was contrary to my experience with my adoptive brother: although he was never a well-behaved child or adult, my parents would never have thought of ending the adoption.

By the late 1980s, my personal and practice experience converged and energized my interest in adoption-related research. I was completing my doctorate in sociology at that time; my newfound skills in research methods and statistics led to several projects and grant activities. My first focus of research was the difficulty of adoption disruption, relating to my disappointing practice experience. Subsequently, when it became apparent that most of these adoptions remain intact and do not disrupt (over 80%), I began to collaborate and study the intact adoptive family with my friend and colleague James Rosenthal. Even though many adoptions remain intact, these are at-risk children and families due to the multiple issues that both the children and families must face as a new family system.

This book is another step in the effort to understand successful adoptive families. As I understand a little more about the uniqueness of this type of family or read a family's life story, I am moved both emotionally and intellectually. Although I have learned a great deal about adoption there is still much to learn. I hope the information presented here can be used to promote policies and practices that help adopted children, the families that raise them, and the professionals who work with them.

Acknowledgments

There are many people to thank in the development of this book. First and foremost, I thank the families who shared part of their lives with me for 4 years. This study would not have happened without their cooperation and their willingness to spend several hours filling out forms and participating in interviews.

Second, I thank the many research assistants who worked for me: at the University of Iowa (UI), Hwi Ja Canda, Cynthia Keeley, David Strabala, Mary Brown (aka Mary Adams), Mark Haines Simeon, Laura Hill, Maryann Basista, and Shannon Cooper, and at Case Western Reserve University (CWRU), Mandel School of Applied Social Sciences (MSASS), Linda Persse, Jane Sibley and Daniela Schmidt. Thank you all for your hard work and effort.

Third, several students completed thesis or research projects that directly and indirectly influenced this manuscript: at UI, Mary Adams, Kelly Corcran-Rumppe, and Karin Mckeone, and at MSASS, Kathy Franz. Your ideas inspired me.

Fourth, several colleagues reviewed chapters and read versions of the manuscript. Many thanks to James Rosenthal from the University of Oklahoma, Elizabeth Tracy and Elizabeth Robinson from CWRU, Kathy Franz from Northeast Ohio Adoption Services, and Karen Rosenberg for reading early drafts. Also, much appreciation to the staff from the UI School of Social Work who assisted with drafts of questionnaires, transcription of interviews, and typing of written comments. Beth Bruder from the Communications and Marketing Department staff at MSASS was invaluable in generating graphs and figures. My multitalented Administrative Assistant, Theresa Lydonne Wilson, did an exceptional job with the final draft of the manuscript.

Fifth, I thank Marge Corkery and the Iowa Department of Human Services. They helped in getting the project initiated and supported continued efforts at data collection.

Sixth, numerous colleagues have helped me as I endeavored to make the research useful to the field of adoption. I appreciate the support and insight of Jean Young, Anne Gruenewald, Karen Rosenberg, Kay Donley, Regina Kupecky, Drenda Lakin and Kathy Franz.

Special thanks are in order to Mary Adams. In addition to the contribution of her thesis work, she drafted her daughters Jennifer and Sarah to help with data entry. She also collected money from her extended family to pay for postage costs one year when there were no funds. Without her efforts, there would not have been a third year of the project.

1

The Study in Context

INTRODUCTION

Adoption is a unique experience. It is both a legal event and a lifelong process. There have been major changes in adoption practice in the last 20 years. In general, adoption practice has changed from finding infants for infertile couples to include finding an adoptive family who can meet the needs of a special child. With these changes has come an emphasis on the adoption of older and special needs children. While thousands of special needs children are adopted annually, the practice of placing children with special needs in adoptive homes is relatively new in child welfare. There is still much to be learned about placing the older and special needs child in an adoptive family.

This book reports on a longitudinal study of special needs adoption. It is one of the few books that focus on this population. It was written to help practitioners, policymakers, researchers, and adoptive parents improve their understanding of the complicated issues in special needs adoption. It is organized into 8 chapters. Chapter 1 examines the historical and research contexts and offers a conceptual model for organizing the information about issues in special needs adoption. Chapter 2 provides details of the study sample and design, including who dropped out and who participated in interviews.

Chapter 3 gives an overview of families and children during the 4 years of the study. Chapter 4 highlights the experiences of siblings separated and kept together in adoptive placements. Chapter 5 presents the adoption experiences and outcomes for children with a preadoptive history of physical and sexual abuse. Chapter 6 examines the issue of social support and the adoptive family.

Chapter 7 discusses practice, policy, and program implications. Chapter 8 discusses adoption issues as we approach the next century.

THE HISTORICAL CONTEXT

Although there is a voluntary reporting system, there is no precise information on the number of adoptions since the federal government stopped collecting adoption statistics. Collecting adoption statistics is also complicated because about half of the adoptions in the United States are completed through attorneys, and this information is not gathered routinely by any monitoring system. It is estimated that 2% to 5% of American families include an adopted child (Bachrach, 1986; Bachrach et al., 1989; Moorman & Hernandez, 1989; Stolley, 1993).

Actually, two different groups of children enter a family through adoption. First, there are children who are adopted as infants, over half the children placed for adoption. Second, there are children with special needs who are adopted. While there is no national definition, and each state decides its own definition, children with special needs include children who are older when placed for adoption, who are members of a sibling group, who have physical, emotional, or behavior difficulties, and who are of mixed or minority race. It is estimated that each year over 35,000 children in need of an adoptive home have one or more special needs (Tatara, 1988).

Many special needs children have traumatic histories with the biological family and have spent time in the public child welfare system before entering the adoptive family. This is typically not the experience of infant adoptees. The experiences of these two groups of adopted children, the infant adoptee compared to the special needs adoptee, share many similarities at different points in their life cycle. Also, there is increased recognition of the special needs of some infant adoptees as they get older. However, there are also significant differences between them (see Groze & Rosenberg, forthcoming).

The children with special needs, many who were victims of foster care drift, were the target of the Child Welfare Act of 1980, and federal demonstration service projects were developed for them through Adoption Opportunities to promote permanency through adoption. Since the passage of this landmark legislation, the adoption of special needs children has received intermittent negative media attention. First, there was the difficulty with adoption disruption. Disruption refers to ending the adoptive placement before legalization. Disruption rates from 7% to 60% have been reported (Groze, 1986; Kagan & Reid, 1986; Rosenthal, Schmidt, & Conner, 1988; Barth & Berry, 1988); the range in rates is attributed to the age of the child, with older children who have behavioral and emotional problems experiencing higher rates of disruption. The most commonly used estimate is that about 15% of adoptions disrupt (Barth & Berry, 1988), which means that most adoptions remain intact.

Next, negative attention focused on families who were dissolving the adoption. Dissolution means legally terminating the adoption after it has been finalized. Few studies examine the dissolutions; many studies place disruptions and dissolutions in the same category. The best estimate is that less than 2% of adoptive placements dissolve after finalization (Barth, 1988; Rosenthal, Schmidt, & Conner, 1988;

Schaffer & Lindstrom, 1990). However, the highly publicized cases and the focusing of television stories and shows on this issue exaggerate the extent of the problem.

Third, the media began to focus on the lawsuits in adoption. Increasing numbers of families began returning to agencies seeking information and supportive services as a result of adoption-related difficulties. Initially, families had difficulty getting their needs met, and some filed lawsuits against agencies to secure services and information. Many agencies reexamined their policies and practice on releasing information and began answering requests for postadoption services as an extension of the adoption services they were providing. However, the lack of adequate funding for these services precluded the development of formal, intensive postadoption programs. At the same time, experience from working with adoptive families highlighted the need for specific post-adoption services with service requirements that vary significantly from one family to another. Most important, agencies found that when sufficient supports were not available, the family reached a critical stage where ending the adoptive placement was a distinct possibility. There are several ways to end the adoptive placement: disruption or dissolution, which is permanent, and out-of-home placement, which may or may not be permanent. While there are no accurate estimates of the number of out-of-home placements of adopted children, several studies suggest that adopted children are overrepresented in residential centers (Brodzinsky, 1987; Piersma, 1987; Rogeness, Hoppe, & Macedo, 1988). So media attention focused on the unmet needs for information and services of adoptive families; professionals became concerned about the number of adopted children in residential treatment.

Most recently, critiques of adoption have questioned the notion that "every child is adoptable," given the influx of children into the child welfare system from the drug and human immunodeficiency virus (HIV) epidemics. There are a new emphasis and dialogue on returning to group and institutional care for children. Thus, once again, parents, advocates, practitioners, and researchers are being called upon to justify adoption.

Not all media attention has been negative. Indeed, the media have played an active role in recruitment and have also focused on positive adoption stories. In some ways, even the negative media attention helps adoption practitioners and researchers to focus on the questions that are not answered. At this point, while several large studies have focused on adoptive families at specific times, little has been provided about what happens over time. This lack of information provides the research context for this project.

THE RESEARCH CONTEXT

The 1980s and the early 1990s generated many studies that confirmed and challenged clinical or qualitative judgments as well as refined the theory and practice of special needs adoption. This pool of research provides much of the support for current policy and practice. However, there are some difficulties with this adoption research. For instance, several studies use ex post facto designs involving secondary analysis of case records (Zwimpfer, 1983; Groze, 1986), surveys or interviews from social workers (Rosenthal, Schmidt, & Conner, 1988; Coyne & Brown, 1985; Kagan & Reid, 1986), or interviews with adoptive parents (Schmidt, Rosenthal, & Bombeck, 1988; Barth & Berry, 1988). In ex post facto studies, it is not possible to distinguish between cause and effect. For example, the perception of parents who have experienced a disrupted adoption may result in a more negative appraisal of the child because it occurs after the fact rather than assessing their perceptions before a negative outcome occurs. The use of case records may reflect bias; they often lack all the variables that are necessary to understand the issue under study because they are produced for other purposes besides research.

Other studies have relied on qualitative or clinical work as the methodology (McNamara & McNamara, 1990; Melina, 1986; Groze, Haines-Simeon, & McMillen, 1992). While these studies are often rich in detail, they lack scientific rigor and the ability to generalize. Part of the problem is their reliance on very small samples that are not chosen randomly or only on clinical populations that are experiencing difficulties.

In an attempt to strengthen methodology, some studies have employed two or more methods of collecting data, also known as methods triangulation (Webb et al., 1966; Smith, 1975; Bailey, 1987). However, even studies that employ methods triangulation suffer from many of the shortcomings mentioned previously, such as ex post facto designs or different data collection techniques at each research site (Barth & Berry, 1988; Partridge, Hornby, & McDonald, 1986; Urban Systems Research & Engineering [USRE], 1985).

Of most concern is the tendency to rely predominantly on cross-sectional data as the basis for policy and practice decisions (Nelson, 1985; Deiner, Wilson, & Unger, 1988; Unger, Deiner, & Wilson, 1988; Rosenthal & Groze, 1990, 1991; Groze & Rosenthal, 1991a, 1991b; Groze, 1992; Rosenthal, Groze, & Aguilar, 1991; Rosenthal et al., 1991; Rosenthal, Groze, & Curiel, 1990). While cross-sectional information can be invaluable for describing phenomena and giving indications of trends, it is also seriously flawed. One cannot conclude from cross-sectional data whether correlates of different variables represent causes or consequences. For example, family rigidity is associated with more negative adoption outcomes (i.e., disruption, less satisfaction, and poor parent/child relations). Several interpretations of this finding are possible. One is that as family flexibility decreases, there is a decrease in parent/child relations. A second interpretation is equally plausible: a decrease in parent/child relations that the family responds to by increasing family rigidity. The first of these two interpretations can be distinguished from the second one only by longitudinal data.

An additional difficulty is that cross-sectional studies cannot capture changes over time. Longitudinal studies provide the richest understanding of adoptive family life. A cross-sectional study is similar to a photograph while a longitudinal study is like a moving picture. While both have merits, following families over time provides a clear context for understanding families at any one time.

Longitudinal Studies in Adoption

There have been some retrospective studies of adult adoptees (Cardoret et al., 1990; Cadoret & Stewart, 1991) and several prospective studies of infant adoptees completed in Europe (Bohman, 1971; Bohman & Sigvardsson, 1980, 1982; Seglow, Pringle, & Wedge, 1972) and Canada (Lipman, Offord, Racine, & Boyle, 1992; Offord et al., 1992; Lipman et al., 1993). Few prospective longitudinal studies in adoption have been conducted in America. One of the first was conducted in Iowa (Skeels, 1938; Skodak, 1939; Skodak & Skeels, 1945, 1949). One hundred white children who were placed for adoption under the age of 6 months participated in a study over 10 years. The authors indicated that fewer than 3% of the adoptees had difficulty dealing with their adoption in early adolescence. The cognitive development of the children remained above average throughout childhood, latency, and adolescence. They suggest that a child's development and growth are most affected by a combination of security and an intellectually stimulating environment.

At approximately the same time in Chicago, Elonen and Schwartz (1969) began a longitudinal study of 43 children, most of whom had been placed as infants. Intelligence tests were conducted before adoptive placement, children were periodically assessed until their 6th birthday, and final testing occurred after the adoptees were 16. Of particular interest was whether adopted children were more susceptible to emotional and behavior problems. The major finding was that most of the adoptees adjusted well, and adoption status was not a causative factor in the development of emotional problems. One difficulty that did emerge was that a large number of children had school difficulties. In trying to understand the differences between children with difficulties and children with no difficulties, one factor that the authors speculated contributed to difficulties was high parental expectations.

Over 20 years later, 2 studies, 1 in Texas (Loehlin, Willerman, & Horn, 1985, 1987) and 1 in Colorado (DeFries et al., 1981; Plomin & DeFries, 1983, 1985; LaBuda et al., 1986), employed a longitudinal design to further explore issues of genetics and heredity in adopted children. Plomin and colleagues tested children and families when children were ages 1 through 4. Data were collected on about 200 adoptive families who adopted infants and 200 control families. In general, the data suggest that genetics and heredity play a larger role in cognitive ability and temperament than does family environment.

During approximately the same time, Loehlin and colleagues (1985, 1987) reported on 181 adopted children participating in a study at 2 different times over a 10-year period. All children were placed for adoption as infants, and families were middle-class, white families. Results suggest genetics play a modest role in the personality development of the adopted children.

In addition to studies on intellectual and personality development, several studies have followed the progress of children in transracial placements. Feigelman and Silverman (1983) drew their sample from lists of adoptive parent groups, a large adoption agency, and names of adoptive families who were known to leaders of parent groups. Sixty percent of their sample responded to their survey (N=737) during the first year, and 7 years later about 68% of families who could be located participated in the second part of the study (N=372). Results suggest that the adoption of children by fertile parents was as positive as adoption by infertile parents, adjustments of transracial adoptees were similar to adjustments of inracial adoptees, and single parents were as good a resource for adoptive placement as were two-parent families.

In related studies of race and adoption, Simon, Altstein, and Melli (1977, 1981, 1987, 1994) have followed children and families who have adopted transracially. The initial study (1977) included 206 families living in 5 different cities in the Midwest; most had adopted an African-American child. In the second stage of the study (1981), 71% of the original families participated. Surveys, rather than interviews, were used in the second wave of the study. In the third stage of the study (1987), when children were in adolescence, about half the original families were involved in the investigation. In the last stage of the study, Simon, Altstein, and Melli (1994) focused on the children, who were young adults at the time of data collection. At this stage, 55 transracially adopted children, 30 birth children, and 13 inracially (white) children participated in interviews.

In general, reports comparing white and transracial adoptees remained positive over time. Through the adolescent years, transracial adoptees saw themselves as having the same type of family relationship as other children, did not evidence self-esteem or racial identity difficulties, and seemed to be performing well in most areas of their lives. In addition, parents and children agreed on these issues. As young adults, the transracially adopted children had shifted close friendships from white to nonwhite peers, and after adolescence relations with parents and siblings improved dramatically. Results from the children as young adults did not negate the positive outcomes reported earlier.

In addition to studies on race and adoption, Hoopes (1982) conducted a longitudinal study comparing adoptive and biological families. Beginning in 1962, 260 white families who had adopted white infants and 68 biological families with birth children participated in the study. Data were collected in 2 periods. During the second stage of the Hoopes study, about 69 families participated in various stages of the data collection.

Initially, Hoopes indicated that adoptive parents presented themselves as more affectionate and permissive than biological parents. She suggests that adoptive parents may have tried to "prove" they were better parents. There were more similarities than differences between adoptive and biological parents during the first 5 years. Over time, parents were consistent in their child rearing attitudes. Parents who were viewed as controlling and dominating tended to raise children who were not self-confident and who were dependent or acting out. In addition, adopted children were evaluated as having more behavior problems in school than their nonadopted peers.

Studies on nontraditional family forms have also been conducted. Shireman and Johnson (1976, 1985, 1986; Shireman, 1988), focusing on the single parent, studied adoptive families when the children were ages 4, 8, and 14. The children were adopted as infants. Overall they were very positive about adoption by single parents. Children were beginning to separate from the family in early adolescence, peer relations were an area of strength, and there were no noticeable self-esteem difficulties.

Finally, of longitudinal studies published in adoption, only one has focused on special needs children. Westhues and Cohen (1990) examined the issue of disruption. Fifty eight families who had adopted 79 children participated in the study. Family functioning data were collected before adoptive placement; data from the dependent variable of case outcome were collected 1 year after adoptive placement. Results suggest that the father's perception of family functioning is a better indicator of placement stability than reports from the adoptive mother. In addition, those couples who showed that they were high in expectations and indicated infertility as their reason for adoption were more likely to disrupt the placement.

The longitudinal studies conducted are quite limited. Most focus on children adopted as infants; only one focuses on the child with special needs. Many studies have not relied on random assignment to obtain their original samples, calling into question the generalizability of their results. Sample attrition is a problem with the studies; most do not compare families who drop out to those who remain. In addition, several studies were most interested in issues of genetics and heredity. A comprehensive longitudinal study of older and special needs adoptees would fill a gap in the knowledge base. In addition, a study that employs good sampling and can provide a profile of attrition would be an improvement over previous studies.

THE CONCEPTUAL CONTEXT

The theoretical perspective used is a family systems model. Family problems and difficulties are seen as connected to developmental processes as well as to the task of integrating various family systems. Difficulties can occur during transitional times, such as when the structure of the family and the developmental requirements of the individual child or children do not coincide or when the pace of family reorganization is too fast or too slow such that individual family members are not able to get their needs met inside the family system (Falicov, 1988). As part of this model, it was recognized that in the adoptive family life cycle, adoptive families may encounter more stressors than do other types of family systems (Talen & Lehr, 1984; DiGiulio, 1987; Rosenberg, 1992) and have unique life cycle issues (Rosenberg, 1992). Stressors in the adoptive family include those from the community, those imposed by the service system, and those that the child as a subsystem brings to the family as well as those the family system brings to the new adoptive family system (Barth & Berry, 1988).

The Community as a Stressor

One difficulty for adoptive parents is the lack of role prescriptions (Clingempeel, 1981; Kirk, 1984). In many ways, adoptive parents suffer from role ambiguity, which refers to situations where there are no clear guidelines from the community about how to execute one's role (Patterson, 1988). This can be stressful because the adoptive family may be insecure about parenting, which is not unusual for all new parents. However, it can be more complicated for many adoptive parents who feel that they must be the exceptional parent or perfect parent but lack realistic role models about how a "good adoptive parent" behaves. Even the popular media can portray adoptive parents as martyrs (e.g., "The Baby Jessica Story"[1]) or villains (e.g., "Mommy Dearest"), characterizations that do not help parents define more clearly their role as an adoptive parent. In fact, these media stories can undermine the confidence adoptive families achieve in their roles over time.

A second stressor is the lack of community support. Building a family through adoption lacks the rituals from the larger community that support and strengthen the family. Family rituals serve to strengthen the notion that parents and children belong together and are entitled to each other. For adoptive families of older children, it is not unusual for parents to question entitlement since the child has a history that predated the adoptive placement (Katz, 1986). Birth parents do not often question entitlement. They have the experience of anticipating the child during pregnancy, and the community communicates entitlement through rituals such as baby showers and birth announcements. Birth parents have the experience of birthing the child; the child's history begins with the parents at birth. Adoptive parents do not go through this process. Instead of a sequential progression from anticipation to birth to parenting, adoptive parents must immerse themselves in instant multiple roles (see also McGoldrick & Carter, 1988) without strong community support.

In addition to community rituals, informal support from family, friends, and neighbors for the adoption is important. The lack of informal support is often expressed in subtle ways. It includes suggestions that families "give the children back" when there are difficulties instead of recognizing that difficulties are part of family life and that adopted children may present some unique difficulties. It includes feeling that no one is there who understands or supports you. It also can include the tendency to view adoption as a onetime legal event instead of a lifelong process.

Finally, even the language of popular culture can serve as a stressor to the adoptive family system. When birth parents are labeled "natural parents" or "real parents" in the courts and through the media, the metacommunication is that adoptive parents and adopted children are "unnatural" or "unreal." These labels serve to accentuate status differences between adoptive families and biological families as well as adopted children and birth children. While there has been improvement in the use

---

1. While not a legal adoptive placement, the popular media portrayed this as an adoption story.

of more sensitive language in the recent past, these labels are still the predominant way information is communicated about children and families.

The Service System as a Stressor

The service system is often a stressor to families. First, the adoptive family must deal over an extended period with a child welfare agency in order to become adoptive parents. The process of building a family by adoption starts with recruitment, oftentimes focusing on a specific child or children. Once a family responds to recruitment, a social worker studies the family to determine eligibility. Unfortunately, the approach to home studies has drifted away from a strength-based perspective that uses the home study to explore areas in which the family needs assistance to be successful in adopting. Instead, it has become a vehicle for screening people out of the adoption process, a practice that discourages and disqualifies many families who would be good adoptive families. Inherent in this process has been a white, middle-class bias on what is an "appropriate" adoptive family. The result seems to prejudice low-income, minority, and single-parent families. However, some families survive the process. If the family is judged acceptable, and a child or children are placed in the family, a social worker makes periodic visits to the family so as to supervise the placement until legalization. This prolonged involvement with an agency can become a stressor to the family.

Second, besides the process that can provoke stress in families, other specific agency practices can become stressors. While there has been an increased emphasis on preplacement services, many agencies do not offer enough or sufficient structured training for potential adoptive families. Thus, an additional source of stress becomes insufficient preadoptive placement training (Aldridge & Cautley, 1975; Chestang & Heymann, 1976; Meezan & Shireman, 1982; Nelson, 1985; Katz, 1986; Barth, 1988; Barth & Berry, 1988).

A third source of stress is incomplete information about the child (Nelson, 1985; Schmidt, Rosenthal, & Bombeck, 1988; Groze, 1994). In the recent past, some agencies purposely withheld information about the child. In other cases, records were inadequate or poorly kept, although children had spent a considerable length of time in the child welfare system. Then, almost as common, information was not known at the time of placement but became known later. Sometimes the information was lacking because no one asked, a poor casework practice. Other times, children were not willing or able to share this information until after they had been with an adoptive family for an extended period. The lack of complete information can result in poor matching of children and families and a misassessment of the readiness of a child to make an adoptive attachment, which also places tension on the family system (Unger, Dwarshuis, & Johnson, 1977; Donley, 1990). Whether the information was withheld, poorly recorded, or unavailable, the lack of complete information serves as a stressor.

A fourth source of stress is the lack of adoption-sensitive social services. The shortage of postplacement services that support and assist the family can result in more negative adoption outcomes (Barth et al., 1986; Nelson, 1985; Groze, Young & Corcran-Rumppe, 1991). Adoption is not a time-limited process, and adoption-related issues surface throughout the life cycle (Bourguignon & Watson, 1987, 1989; Winkler et al., 1988; Rosenberg, 1992). Therapeutic expertise that is knowledgeable about both adoption and child welfare issues is unique. Conventional therapy and service-provision methods can be ineffective with adoptive families if adoption issues are ignored or minimized. On the other hand, viewing adoption as the problem or ending the adoption as the solution can undermine the inherent confidence and strengths of adoptive families. A cadre of practitioners and services that are adoption-sensitive is needed; the lack of these resources serves as an additional source of stress to adoptive families.

A final source of stress is fee structures. Many agencies, including those placing children with special needs, have developed fees for services. While there are both federal and state funds for some services, the mechanism for funding imposes barriers on the agency that passes on, albeit inadvertently, the barriers to families. For example, many states do not support a program of recruitment; oftentimes, recruitment is considered one of many activities required of adoption workers. Also, many states do not pay for a home study unless it results in the adoptive placement of a child. The result is that agencies can expend a great deal of time and effort on recruitment and home studies without financial reimbursement. In order to balance the budget, costs associated with this component of adoption activities are passed on to the adoptive family. Fee practices are a disincentive to adopt for lower-income and minority families (McKenzie, 1993), whether the fee is for a home study or for postlegal services. Even when based on a sliding scale, the use of fees to support adoption services can create an additional source of stress to the family (McKenzie, 1993).

Related to the issue of fees are subsidies. Adoption subsidies were created to help families where finances could pose a barrier to adoption or when the needs of the child were greater than the resources families had available. By far, subsidies are evaluated as the service most helpful to adoptive parents. However, several problems with the subsidy program create additional stress to families. First, as a matter of practice, adoption workers do not discuss subsidy until a family makes a commitment to adopt. Thus, some families who might be willing to adopt if subsidy arrangements are discussed early are discouraged from pursuing the adoption. Part of this reluctance is the belief by agency workers and supervisors that people would choose to adopt because they know that money is available, not because they have the child's best interest in mind. When parents are knowledgeable and ask about subsidy, they are viewed as suspect. Of course, anyone who has parented children knows that even enhanced subsidies do not begin to cover the cost for raising children.

Second, there are problems when state policy dictates that adoption subsidy rates must be lower than foster care rates. This policy contradicts an emphasis on permanency; if anything, adoption subsidy should be at, or higher than, the foster care rate. Adoption subsidies should not be reduced from the foster care rate because they save the federal and state government in administrative costs once the child is adopted. By promoting policies that are positive and support subsidy, issues around finances as a source of stress could be reduced for many adoptive families.

The Family System as a Stressor

Several family system stressors put families at risk of adoption instability. First, there is the problem of high parental expectations (Rosenthal, Schmidt, & Conner, 1988; Partridge, Hornby, & McDonald, 1986; USRE, 1985). High parental expectations can develop for the "dream" or "fantasy" child. Imbued with popular myths about adoptees (Sandmaier, 1988), parents develop dreams and expectations about the child or children they adopt. These dreams and expectations can be reinforced by socioeconomic status, with middle- and upper-class families holding rigid, high aspirations for their children. Oftentimes, parents imagine the child will be a loving, happy "orphan" willing and grateful to be adopted. In professional career families, there may be implicit or explicit expectations that the child will pursue a similar career path. Clearly, with many special needs children being adopted who have severe emotional and behavioral problems as well as an array of significant learning difficulties, these expectations will not be congruent with reality.

Second, families that are not flexible have a reduced capacity to deal with the stress of integrating an adopted child in the family, which puts the adoptive placement at greater risk (Boneh, 1979; Cohen, 1984). To accomplish family integration, the adoptive family and the family system the adopted child brings to the family must change to develop a third system, much like the experiences of blended families (Carter & McGoldrick, 1988). When a family system is too rigid, the tasks associated with integration become problematic.

Third, families without adequate support systems are at greater risk for a range of difficulties than are families with well-developed support systems. Social support serves as a buffer against stressors (Gore, 1981; House, 1981; Caplan, 1974). Feeling supported and cared for decreases the negative effects of all stressful life events. The absence of support can present environmental risks to a family (Garbarino, 1983). Froland (1979) suggested that social support systems can help a family in defining a problem, in seeking the appropriate help through the informal system of referral, in buffering the stress, and in enhancing the effects of professional intervention by providing support before, during and after professional assistance.

The Child Subsystem as a Stressor

Many children who enter families through special needs adoption programs have an extensive history with the birth family as well as the child welfare system. Often, their experience with the birth family involves abuse or neglect. Attachment difficulties (Barth & Berry, 1988; Kirgan, Goodfield, & Campana, 1982; Aber & Allen, 1987), behavior problems (Yarrow, cited in Sack & Dale, 1982; Rutter, 1972; Yates, 1981; Green, 1978), and learning problems (Sandmaier, 1988) are the result of spending formative years in an abusive or neglectful family. These difficulties are stressors to the adoptive family system.

In addition, the individual coping style of the child can be a stressor (Barth & Berry, 1988). To create familiarity in the new family, it is not unusual for the child(ren) to promote coalitions and triangulation to diffuse intimacy and increase their control in this family environment. Sometimes the strongest coalition is between siblings; other times, they target one parent in a two-parent family to build a coalition against others in the family system. While this negatively affects family functioning, it is the child's attempt to retain control over the situation. This is one coping style that children developed as survivors in the child welfare system (Donley, 1990).

Relatedly, children may not have developed the interpersonal and social skills to live successfully with others or may not have a very good idea about how families function. This may be particularly true if the child has spent an extended period of time in group or residential care. They often have questions about boundaries: who is inside the family system, who is outside the family system, and what is the appropriate way to relate to each other inside the family system? For sexually abused children, they may not have good boundaries about their bodies, both with people inside the family and with people outside the family. The physically abused and neglected child may not respect personal space, including property. They may hoard items or not place much value on property. Boundary ambiguity may create or exacerbate demands on the developing family system.

Children also may have issues around roles (Reitz & Watson, 1992). Sometimes the issue is role conflict, particularly for the child who has been the parental child. They may not be able to make the transition back to the role of a child. There also may be role ambiguity. This may be particularly true for the child who has been in multiple placements and has occupied several role positions. For example, the child may have been the oldest child in the birth family, the youngest in the first foster family, and a middle child in the current adoptive family. Occupying several role positions in several family systems can be very confusing to the child. Some behavior and adjustment of the child to the family system may be an attempt to discover his or her role in the family system.

Resources to the Adoptive Family

While the preceding discussion outlines stressors, any of these stressors can be changed to become resources to the adoptive family system. For example, working with the media to present accurate, positive depictions and role models of adoptive parents can reduce role ambiguity. While not having an immediate effect, over time such a strategy can create a more positive climate for adoptive families and children. Creating rituals to celebrate the different components of adoptive family life, such as the decision to adopt, the first meeting between parents and child, or the date of joining the family, can strengthen the family. Promoting these rituals and teaching the community about the purposes of such rituals can assist in garnering community support. As part of public education and continuing education for professionals, helping people to understand the power of language is essential. People need informal supports and to be taught to use words to discuss adoption that are empowering and sensitive as well as language that communicates support for this unique type of family system.

Better agency policy and practice can strengthen families. Returning to the use of home studies for case planning to help a family in becoming an adoptive family, rather than screening out, would make more families available to adopt as well as make families feel less anxious during the adoption process. Enhancing and promoting subsidies can reduce or eliminate financial barriers. An array of preplacement and postplacement services that are free, accessible and adoptive-sensitive need to be developed, including training, support, and an assortment of therapies. As part of these services, families' skills can be increased, such as improving families' ability to deal with behavioral and emotional problems that children manifest, assisting families to become more flexible and patient, helping families develop realistic expectations and inner resources on which to draw when problems arise, and working with the family to develop strong systems of formal and informal social support. These family system interventions can reduce the risk of disruption, dissolution and out-of-home placement in adoption (Smith & Sherwen, 1983; Cohen, 1984; Partridge, Hornby, & MacDonald, 1986; Gil, 1978; Fanshel, 1962; Feigelman & Silverman, 1983; Groze, 1986; Kagan & Reid, 1986; Deiner, Wilson, & Unger, 1988; USRE, 1985; Westhues & Cohen, 1990; Nelson, 1985; Barth & Berry, 1988).

For the adopted child, Chestang and Heymann (1976) emphasize children's preparation in planning for an adoption. They suggest that children can adequately identify their own needs and wants in a family. Essential for adoption preparation are clarification of adoption, explanation of the difference between adoption and foster care, and dealing with a child's fear and resistance to change. Besides adoption preparation, many children may need assistance in both improving their coping skills as well as improving their capacity to live in a family. There should be no assumption that a child can cope with family relationships and dynamics or that the child is predisposed to familiarity and comfort with family relationships. Indeed, many life experiences of children are contrary to this assumption. Practice families that offer visitation and the opportunity for children to interact in a family environment, particularly for children who have been in group or institutional care, can be an asset. Thoughtful consideration of these issues must be undertaken as part of assisting the child for successful adoption. Table 1.1 presents the resources and stressors outlined in the previous discussion.

Table 1.1
Resources and Stressors to the Adoptive Family System

Stressors	Resources
Community	**Community**
Role ambiguity	Accurate, positive role models in media
Lack of support/rituals	Creation of community & family rituals
Popular language	Adoption sensitive language
Lack of informal support	Public education about adoption
	Normalizing adoption
	Increase informal support systems
Service System	**Service System**
Adoption process	Focus on empowering families
Home study	Focus on family strengths
Lack of pre-adoptive training	Sufficient, accessible training
Incomplete info on children	Better record-keeping, casework
Fees	Eliminate all fees
Lack of adoption	Develop adoption sensitive
sensitive services	service system & therapists
Family System	**Family System**
Unrealistic expectations	Sufficient, accessible training
Low flexibility	Skill building to enhance adaptability
Inadequate support systems	Support system intervention
	Array of pre & post placement services
Child Subsystem	**Child Subsystem**
Attachment difficulties	Individual intervention
Behavior problems	Adoption preparation
Learning problems	Practice families
Poor coping skills	
Poor interpersonal	
and social skills	
Poor family living skills	
Role confusion	

A FAMILY MODEL FOR ADOPTIVE FAMILIES:
BALANCING STRESSORS AND RESOURCES

Stress occurs in all families. Crisis occurs in a family when existing resources are not sufficient to meet current demands. Crisis is characterized by family disorganization or disruptiveness where old patterns and capabilities are no longer adequate, and change is necessary (Patterson, 1988). Crisis is very uncomfortable to families and may threaten the integrity of the family system (i.e., the family may break up). The Family Adjustment and Adaptation Response (FAAR) Model, developed out of crisis theory (Patterson, 1988), is one way to organize the stressors and resources previously outlined. This is a family system model that posits that all families use capabilities (resources and coping behaviors) to meet the demands (stressors and strains) to maintain family balance. When stress occurs, the family musters the resources to deal with it. In a sense, it balances the stressor with a resource. Crisis occurs when there are too many stressors and not enough resources, or when there is a buildup of stressors such that the family cannot accommodate quickly enough to garner its resources. So, both the lack of resources or an overload of stressors can place a family in crisis.

Besides using this model as a way of understanding difficulties in adoptive families, adoption life cycle theory can be used to predict certain times when adoptive families may experience stress that could lead to crisis. Knowing this can help families more effectively plan for resource development and allocation.

In applying the life cycle model to adoptive families, the first stressful phase is easy to identify. Initially, for many adoptive families there is the "honeymoon period" of transition when the adopted child is not too challenging to the family system. The honeymoon period eventually ends and usually sparks some family crisis. Crisis occurs in an adoptive family when children and families are faced with the concrete tasks of integration. Most likely, the process of integration for an adoptive family may involve several honeymoon periods followed by crisis. The successful resolution of 1 crisis makes it more likely that the family will be successful in later crises. However, some families never encounter a honeymoon period and children immediately begin adoptive family life by challenging the task of integration.

Other crises may be provoked by anniversary dates (Rosenberg, 1992). Birthdays, placement dates, crises or traumas that occurred on specific dates or seasons prior to adoptive placement, the birth date of a birth parent or sibling not placed in the same home-all these can trigger stress or crisis in the adoptive family. Helping the family understand these unique issues for their child can assist them in successfully navigating the issues as they encounter them.

Finally, crises may be provoked as part of normative development experiences or life circumstances: entering or changing schools, the eldest child leaving home, marital discord, school failure, and so on. Of course, these are many of the same events that can provoke crises or difficulties in other families. It is important to keep in mind that there are both similarities and differences in the multitude of family systems that make up the fabric of American family life.

Understanding both the unique life cycle of the adoptive family and the issues that can contribute to stress and crisis can help families normalize their experiences. For example, helping families understand the child's history provides an opportunity for the family to try to understand how these experiences affect the child and family presently. Verbal discussion, written information, and community resources assist the family in understanding how the child's behaviors and responses are survival skills the child has developed in response to his or her history. This understanding allows the family to depersonalize the child's behavior. The parent(s) can then move forward to identifying what they can do to help the child and family to function in a way that is more satisfying. Also, by normalizing that the adoptive families' experience is similar to that of other adoptive families of special needs children, issues can become detoxified.

2

The Research Study

THE DESIGN

This was a longitudinal study initiated in the spring of 1990 and completed in the summer of 1993. This study attempts to improve existing adoption research methodology in the following ways:

- obtaining a random sample of subsidized adoption cases in the original sampling strategy;

- providing 4 years of data on the experiences of children and families in intact adoptive placements after legal finalization;

- providing trend data on children's behavior that can be compared to normative data as well as providing data about how children's behavior changes over time; and

- providing trend data on family functioning and dynamics that can be compared to normative data as well as providing data about how family functioning changes over time.

It is anticipated that this research will assist parents, practitioners, policy-makers, and researchers in developing a better understanding of issues and dynamics in special needs adoptive placements over time.

RESEARCH INSTRUMENTS

The survey instruments used in the study were adapted from the same instrument used with other midwestern states (Rosenthal & Groze, 1992). Several other instruments with national norms were used.

To assess family functioning, the Family Adaptability and Cohesion Evaluation Scales (FACES III) were used (Olson, Portner, & Lavee, 1985). FACES provides information about family cohesion and adaptability. Family cohesion is the bond that family members have toward one another. Family adaptability is the ability of a family system to change in response to situational and developmental stress. These two dimensions of family functioning are integrated into a Circumplex Model (Olson, Russell, & Sprenkle, 1979, 1980, 1983; Olson, 1989).

Ratings of children's behaviors were obtained by the Child Behavior Checklist (CBC) developed by Achenbach and Edelbrock (1983). The portion of the CBC used in this research was the list of 113 behavior problems with the 1991 scoring for the CBC (Achenbach, 1991).

Attachment measures were developed from two different theoretical perspectives (see Groze & Rosenthal, 1993; Groze, 1992). One perspective, which developed from research in juvenile delinquency, is known as a social control perspective (Hirschi, 1969). It includes the dimensions of communication, shared activities, and trust. Added to these dimensions were items measuring getting along, respect, and closeness. The other perspective is ethological, growing out of the theory and research of Bowlby and colleagues (Bowlby, 1969, 1973, 1988; Main, Kaplan, & Cassidy, 1985; Main & Weston, 1981). In measuring attachment, Waters and Deane (1985) recommend consideration of behavioral, affective, and cognitive. Following Johnson and Fein's (1991) recommendations that behavioral clusters, rather than single items, may be best suited for describing attachment, both anxious-ambivalent and anxious-avoidant patterns via subscales were created. Indicators were chosen based on face validity considerations from the Child Behavior Checklist. Reliability (alpha) of the anxious-ambivalent scales was .74 while that of the anxious-avoidant scale was .64 (Groze & Rosenthal, 1993). The anxious-*ambivalent* scale consists of the following: in the affective domain-cries a lot and whining; in the cognitive domain-cannot sit still, restless, or hyperactive, clings to adults or too dependent, and easily jealous; and in the behavioral domain-complains of loneliness and feels or complains that no one loves him or her. The anxious-*avoidant* scale comprises the following: in the affective domain-shy or timid, withdrawn, and does not get involved with others; in the cognitive domain-cruelty, bullying or meanness to others, physically attacks people, and threatens people; and in the behavioral domain-fears certain animals, situations, or places other than school, self-conscious or easily embarrassed.

In the assessment of social support, a social network map (Tracy & Whittaker, 1990; Tracy, 1990) was employed in the interview process. The social network map examines both the structure and function of social networks. It collects information about the size and composition of the network, the extent that the various network members provided differing types of support, and the nature of relations within the network (stability of the network, reciprocity, and frequency of contact). Although originally designed for an individual, the family was engaged in a problem-solving process to decide as a group who were the 15 most important members of their social network.

THE SAMPLE

In the spring of 1990, a systematic sample was drawn by selecting every other family from the list of subsidized adoptions provided by the Iowa Department of Human Services. In sibling placements, 1 sibling was randomly chosen as the focus of the study. The first mailing was followed 30 days later by a second mailing. Only children living in the home whose adoptions were finalized and who were receiving subsidy are included in this report. At the time of the initial study there were approximately 560 families caring for about 947 children. Two hundred eighty surveys were mailed. The response rate of about 70% (199 families) is excellent for a mailed survey assessment.

In the spring of 1991, the 199 families who responded the first year were recontacted to participate in the study for a second year. One hundred ninety-six families or 98% of families were successfully contacted. One hundred thirty-eight families responded to the mailing. The response rate for completed questionnaires for the second year was about 68% (133 of 196 families), comparable to the response rate for the first year.

In the spring of 1992, the 133 families who responded the second year were recontacted to participate in the study for a third year. One hundred twenty-nine families or 97% of families were successfully contacted. One hundred four families responded to the mailing. The response rate for completed questionnaires for the third year was about 80% (104 of 129 families), much better than the response rate for the previous 2 years.

In the spring of 1993, the 104 families who responded the third year were recontacted to participate in the study for a fourth year. Seventy-one families responded to the mailing for a response rate of 68%. Besides completing surveys, families were asked to participate in an interview process. While 46 families agreed to be interviewed, only 44 (62% of the sample from year 4) could be located during the interview process.

This report is based on the responses of 71 families who participated in all four years of the study (about 25% of the original sample drawn). This study builds on previous research that used the same instruments for a large, cross-sectional study (Rosenthal & Groze, 1992).

How Similar are the Samples to the Population of Subsidized Cases?

Table 2.1 examines the representativeness of the samples for each year by comparing selected child demographic characteristics. During the first 3 years of the study, there are no statistically significant differences between the population and the samples for child's age at the time of the study, gender of the child, and race of the child. During the fourth year, there is a significant difference between the sample (mean=12.5) and population (mean=13.7) for child age; results suggest that older

Table 2.1
Comparing Population and Sample Characteristics
for the Iowa Subsidized Adoption Study

	All Subsidized in Iowa in 1990 (N= 947)	Parental Responses Year 1 (N=199)	Parental Responses Year 2 (N=133)	Parental Responses Year 3 (N=104)	Parental Responses Year 4 (N=71)
Age of Child at Time of Study					
Mean	10.7	10.3	11.4	12.1	12.5
Std. Dev.	4.3	4.3	4.2	4.0	3.8
N	(945)	(198)	(131)	(102)	(69)
		t=1.58,p-ns	t=.96,p=nsd	t=.29,p=ns	t=2.35,p<.01
Gender of Child					
Male	52.7%	50.5%	50.8%	48.5%	49.3%
Female	47.3%	49.5%	49.2%	51.1%	50.7%
N	(866)	(198)	(132)	(101)	(17)
		z=.56,p=ns	z=.41,p=ns	z=.80,p=ns	z=.55,p=ns
Race of Child					
White	86.4%	83.0%	82.6%	85.1%	81.7%
Nonwhite	13.6%	17.0%	17.4%	14.9%	18.3%
N	(911)	(194)	(132)	(101)	(71)
		z=1.16,p=ns	z=1.09,p=ns	z=.35,p=ns	z=.99,p=ns

Note: Percents were compared using the difference of proportions and t-tests were used to compare means (see Blalock, 1979). Data for each year were compared to the population of subsidy cases. To determine t-tests for age, the population mean age was increased by 1 year for year 2 and 2 years for year 3.

children dropped out of the study by the fourth year. Thus, results are biased toward younger children. However, the comparison data for race and gender suggest that, based on these characteristics, the samples are representative of subsidized adoptions in Iowa during all 4 years.

Who Dropped Out of the Study?

In addition to examining the similarities between the sample and the population, analysis examined who dropped out compared to who remained in all 4 years of the study. Tables 2.2 and 2.3 present child and family demographics for those who remained compared to those who dropped out. While the age of the child at study initiation and the length of time the child has been in the home approached statistical significance (p=.06), the families who dropped out were demographically similar to families who remained in the study.

Table 2.2
Comparing Demographics of Families Who Dropped out
to Those Who Remained for Interval Level Variables

	Dropped Out Mean (SD)	Remained Mean (SD)
Age of Child at time of Study	10.7 (4.4)	9.5 (3.8)#
Age at Placement	4.8 (3.9)	4.8 (3.5)
Length of Time in Adoptive Placement	6.7 (4.2)	5.5 (3.6)#
Age of Adoptive Mother	42.1 (8.0)	41.4 (7.3)
Age of Adoptive Father	43.7 (9.1)	42.6 (7.7)
Average Income	32.5 (15.4)	34.1 (14.1)

p< .05, #p<.10

Comparing Families Participating and Not Participating in Interviews

A number of families agreed to participate in interviews during the fourth year of the study. A comparison can be made between families who participated and families who refused to participate in interviews. Using the same information as used in Tables 2.2 and 2.3, Tables 2.4 and 2.5 compare demographics of families participating in interviews to families who did not participate in interviews. As evident in Tables 2.4 and 2.5, there are no statistically significant differences between interviewed families and families not interviewed. Preadoptive abuse history and behavior problems (internalizing problems, externalizing problems, and total problems) were also examined, with no differences between the two groups.

Table 2.3
Comparing Demographics of Families Who Dropped out
to Those Who Remained for Categorical Variables

	Dropped Out Percent	Remained Percent
Child Sex		
Male	51.2%	48.8%
Female	49.3%	50.7%
Race of Child		
White	83.7%	81.7%
Nonwhite	16.3%	18.3%
Race of Adoptive Mother		
White	91.7%	92.6%
Nonwhite	8.3%	7.4%
Race of Adoptive Father		
White	93.6%	94.4%
Nonwhite	6.4%	5.6%
Education of Adoptive Mother		
Less than high school	8.5%	6.6%
Completed high school	31.4%	29.4%
Some college	35.6%	22.1%
College graduate	18.6%	23.5%
Master's degree or above	5.9%	13.2%
Education of Adoptive Father		
Less than high school	15.0%	11.1%
Completed high school	39.3%	29.6%
Some college	25.2%	22.2%
College graduate	12.1%	18.5%
Master's degree or above	8.4%	18.5%

SO WHAT DOES ALL THIS MEAN?

One indication of good research is the ability to generalize; that is, knowing what we know about the children and the families in the study, with what degree of confidence can we assume that other adoptive families of special needs children experience these same issues? Clearly, we cannot ascertain the experiences of families who dropped out of the study. In addition, results must be tentative about older children because of the bias in sampling attrition toward younger children in the fourth

Table 2.4
Comparing Demographics of Families Who Participated
in Interviews to Families Not Participating
for Interval Level Variables

	Not Interviewed Mean (SD)	Interviewed Mean (SD)
Age of Child at time of Study	9.8 (3.4)	9.4 (4.2)
Age at Placement	4.4 (3.5)	5.1 (3.5)
Length of Time in Adop- tive Placement	6.0 (3.2)	5.1 (3.9)
Age of Adoptive Mother	41.6 (6.8)	41.1 (7.7)
Age of Adoptive Father	41.2 (6.4)	43.9 (8.5)
Average Income	31.1 (14.7)	36.2 (13.6)

No statistically significant differences.

year. However, given the similarities between the population and the sample as well as the similarities between those who remained and those who dropped out of the study, there is some degree of confidence that the information here is relevant for many adoptive families of children with special needs.

A Note of Caution

There are probably differences between Iowa special needs adoption and special needs adoptions in other states. Descriptions of special needs vary by state. Also, Iowa has a small minority population (about 5%). Minority children are overrepresented in the child welfare system in Iowa, similar to other states. However, they still represent a very small proportion of the state population. In addition, Iowa is a midwestern and predominantly rural state. Generalizations to other state populations should be made with caution.

Table 2.5
Comparing Demographics of Families Who Participated in Interviews
to Families Not Participating for Categorical Variables

	Not Interviewed Percent	Interviewed Percent
Child Sex		
Male	46.9%	51.3%
Female	53.1%	48.7%
Race of Child		
White	81.3%	82.1%
Nonwhite	18.8%	17.9%
Race of Adoptive Mother		
White	87.1%	97.3%
Nonwhite	12.9%	2.7%
Race of Adoptive Father		
White	96.0%	93.1%
Nonwhite	4.0%	6.9%
Education of Adoptive Mother		
Less than high school	16.1%	8.1%
Completed high school	38.7%	21.6%
Some college	22.6%	21.6%
College graduate	16.1%	29.7%
Master's degree or above	6.5%	18.9%
Education of Adoptive Father		
Less than high school	16.0%	6.9%
Completed high school	24.0%	34.5%
Some college	16.0%	27.6%
College graduate	16.0%	20.7%
Master's degree or above	28.0%	10.3%

No statistically significant differences.

ANALYSIS TECHNIQUES

Descriptive data of frequencies, percents, means, and standard deviations are reported when appropriate. The primary multivariate techniques used to analyze the data included regression analysis and a repeated measures analysis of variance (MANOVA). A repeated measures design is appropriate when the same variable is measured on several occasions for each participant. Readers interested in more details of MANOVA are referred to Girden (1992).

3

The Families and Children at a Glance and over Time

This chapter presents descriptive information and an analysis of the major trends from the 4 years of the study. Demographic descriptions are presented first. Subsequently, data from the different domains in the life of the family and child are presented. These domains include educational functioning, contact with the biological family, attachment, children's behavior, family functioning, and adoption outcomes. The last section probes changes over time and what variables best predict changes.

DESCRIPTION OF CHILDREN, PARENTS, AND THE HOME[1]

The range of children's ages at time of placement was infancy to 11, with an average age of 4.8 years (SD=3.5); the median age was 5 years. At the time the study began, on average, these children had been in adoptive placements 5.5 years (SD=3.6); the range of time in the home was 1 year to 19 years. The adopted children were reported as white (82%), black (6%), Hispanic (6%), and other (7%). The "other" category was used for biracial children. Thus, approximately 18% were minority children.

The majority of families who adopted were 2-parent families (83%). At the time of adoptive placement, fathers ranged in age from 24 to 56, with a mean of 37 years; mothers ranged in age from 25 to 56, with a mean of 36 years. At the time the study began, the range of fathers' ages was 29 to 63, with a mean of 43 years (SD=7.7). The range of the mothers' ages was 28 to 67, with a mean age of 41.4 years (SD=7.3). Over 90% of the responding parents were white.

The modal education level was high school or general equivalency diploma (GED) for adoptive mothers and fathers. About one-fourth of the mothers were college graduates, and an additional 13% had graduate degrees. About one-fifth of the

---

1. Most of the demographic data was gathered during the first year of the project. Demographic details were elaborated upon in subsequent years.

adoptive fathers were college graduates and an additional one-fifth had graduate degrees. Family income ranged from $10,000 to over $100,000 yearly, with most families earning between $20,000 and $40,000 a year. Most family incomes (45%) increased over the 4 years of the project. Over one-third reported no change in income over the 4 years. However, about one-fifth reported a decrease in income. One family reported substantial financial loss, while most families reported dropping 1 income category (e.g., from making $30,000-$39,999 to making $20,000-$29,999). The vast majority of families who lost income resided in rural areas, likely reflecting the continuing impact of the farm crisis.

Over 80% of the homes had other children in the home. Other children in the home included mostly adopted and biological children, with several homes having a few foster children or a few stepchildren. Forty-five percent of the placements were sibling placements. The sibling placements usually involved placement of 1 other sibling. About 3% of the placements were with relatives.

During the course of the 4 years, approximately 8% of the 71 children ended up in out-of-home placement. However, in all cases families did not dissolve the adoption and were still connected and invested in the adopted child. Thus, 6 children had been in out-of-home placements during the course of the study. By the fourth year, 5 children remained out of the home. A few other children (N=3) left due to turning 18 and being legally able to do so. One of the children not living in the home during the first year had returned home. Of the children not living in the home, 4 were reported to have a major emotional or behavior problem. The other child was reported to have a developmental delay. The children living out of the home were ages 12, 15, 15, 16, and 17.

SPECIAL NEEDS OF THE ADOPTED CHILD

Table 3.1 lists the special needs of the children. Parents reported from 0 to 6 handicaps or special needs, although, on average, parents reported one special need. The most frequent handicaps reported were emotional or behavioral problems (51%), learning disabilities (35%), and developmental difficulties (25%).

Table 3.2 summarizes preadoptive history information. Most children (75%) had been in foster care before adoptive placement. Most of the children had a biological sibling (82.5%), although only about half were placed with a sibling (46.1%). About half (51%) the children were known or suspected to have been sexually abused, and most (76%) were known or suspected to have been physically abused prior to adoptive placement.

Table 3.1
Special Needs or Handicaps of the Adopted Child
as Reported by Adoptive Parents

Blind or vision impaired	4.2%	(n= 3)
Deaf or hearing impaired	1.4%	(n= 1)
Physical handicap	12.7%	(n= 9)
Mental retardation	19.7%	(n=14)
Developmental delays	25.4%	(n=18)
Learning disabilities	35.2%	(n=25)
Chronic medical problem	21.1%	(n=15)
Emotional or behavioral problem	50.7%	(n=36)
Other handicap	14.1%	(n=10)
Number of Handicaps		
range	0-6	
mean	1.8	
standard deviation	1.3	

Table 3.2
Preadoptive History of the Adopted Child

Percent Indicating Placement		
Relative Placement	18.3%	(n=13)
Foster Care	74.6%	(n=53)
Group Home	2.8%	(n= 2)
Psychiatric Hospital	8.5%	(n= 6)
Other Placement	9.9%	(n= 7)
Mistreatment History		
Physical Abuse		
No	24.3%	(n=17)
Yes	47.1%	(n=33)
Suspected	28.6%	(n=20)
Sexual Abuse		
No	49.3%	(n=35)
Yes	23.9%	(n=17)
Suspected	26.8%	(n=19)

EDUCATIONAL FUNCTIONING

During the course of the 4 years, all children who were age-appropriate were attending school, with 1 exception. During the first year, a 13-year-old boy with major emotional and behavioral problems was out of school at the time of the study. By the second year, he was back in school. During the last year of the study several school-related questions were omitted due to space restrictions and the addition of other questions. To examine school trends, data for children who were in school during the entire 4-year period are reported. In other words, if children were too young to be in school during the first year or over the age of 18 during the last year of the study, they were dropped from the analysis of school trends. Trend data for 56 children are reported later.

Information about grades was collected for only 3 years. For the most part, grades were relatively stable, with the majority of children earning a C average over the 3 years. On a 4-point scale, with an A equivalent to 4.0, scores for the 3 years of data collected were 2.5, 2.3 and 2.4, suggesting a consistent grade average. Each year over one-third of the children earned a B average. About half the children were enrolled in special classes, and this percent remained consistent over time. The most common special education classes were for learning disabilities (29%). About 15% of the children were in classrooms for children with emotional and behavioral problems, speech and language classes, and classes for the mentally retarded. Most children were reported to enjoy school, and this proportion decreased slightly over the 4 years (76%, 75%, 65% and 67%). The percent of children who disliked school changed from 6% during year 1 to 10% during year 4, suggesting a few more children disliked it over time, but this was not a substantial change. School trends were also analyzed for differences between males and females; there were no gender differences in educational functioning throughout the 4 years.

While school was not problematic for the most part, several families wrote about concerns they had with the school system. Several parents wrote about the unwilling-ness or inability of some school systems to handle children with attention deficit disorder, and several were concerned that teachers did not know how to deal with an adopted child and his or her special needs in the classroom.

CONTACTS WITH THE BIOLOGICAL FAMILY

Contacts with the biological family and the effects of these contacts on the child and family were probed during years 1, 2, and 4 of the study and are presented in Table 3.3. During the first year, 37% of the children had contact with members of the biological family. This increased to 41% during years 2 and 4. Most often, this contact was with siblings who were not in the adoptive home. In year 1, of the 23 parents who wrote about their adopted child's contact with biological family members, 60% (N=14) had contact with siblings. Most (79%, N=11) had personal contact with

Table 3.3
Adopted Child's Contacts with the Biological Family

Percent Who Had Contacts After Placements

Year 1	36.6
Year 2	41.4
Year 4	40.8

Effects of Contact on Child	Mostly Good	Some Good	Not Much Effect	Mostly Bad
Year 1	23.1	26.9	42.3	7.7
Year 2	27.6	31.0	34.5	6.9
Year 4	31.3	37.5	28.1	3.1

Effects of Contact on Family	Mostly Good	Some Good	Not Much Effect	Mostly Bad
Year 1	23.1	23.1	42.3	11.5
Year 2	30.0	36.7	23.3	10.0
Year 3	26.7	36.7	30.0	6.7

siblings. In 2 cases the contact with the sibling (sisters in both cases) was incidental in that the visit was primarily with the biological mother in one case and with the maternal grandmother in the other case; the siblings just happened to be present during these meetings. Of siblings who maintained contact, most (64%) of the contact was face-to-face. In the remaining cases, contact was made by phone or mail. In one case, contact was only through phone messages delivered through the adoptive parents who acted as intermediaries.

A recurring theme regarding the contact between siblings reflects the bond of love and caring the children have for each other, even though they do not reside in the same home. Sometimes this bond was expressed as a desire to make sure the other is ok. Some adoptive families acknowledged the bond between siblings and made a commitment to facilitating ongoing contact. The following quotations reflect these recurrent themes, evident in the parent's written comments:

In...1989 she asked me if she could see her younger brother so that she could make sure that he was okay.

Claudia[2] worries about her brother. She seems to be satisfied knowing he is happy.

---

2. All names have been changed.

They just want to know how each other is doing.
(About adopted daughter's contact with her biological brother)

We want the children to remain in contact because it was not their fault they were separated and it bothered them not to be together. These contacts are good for the children, and the way they act when they come together is so special. Parting is not easy because it breaks their hearts and ours.

[We] feel it is important to keep . . . siblings in touch with each other. . . . Our two kids still love their younger siblings. And even when the younger kids are adopted by the other couple, they are still going to be their real brother and sister. So it will be important to all of us that they always keep in touch with each other.

Alicia feels very connected to her younger brother and talks about him often.

About 30% of the children who have contact with their biological family have had some personal contact with their biological mother (N=7). In 1 case the adoptive mother contacted the biological mother by mail but terminated contact when the biological mother expressed a desire to send gifts to the children. In 2 of the 7 cases, contact with the mother ended by choice of the child, and in one case contact with the biological mother was discouraged by the adoptive mother. In all cases where contact was terminated, the reason given was that seeing the biological mother was upsetting to the child, as this adoptive mother commented:

After having an opportunity to visit with her biological brother, and incidentally with her biological mother, the child did not request further visits. I have no objections to her seeing him (her brother) but not her mother. It only creates problems and mixes her up. It . . . confused her some when she saw her real mother and we had some problems from this.

The next most frequent contact was with members of the extended biological family (22%, N=5). In one case, the adoptive parents are the child's aunt and uncle. Three children have contact with grandparents (grandmother or both grandparents). Of these 3 children, one child has had contact with a great-grandfather (at the great-grandfather's initiative), but contact has not been maintained because of the grandfather's health. Regarding the other 2 children, 1 did not wish to continue with visits to her grandparents while the other child visits 4 to 5 times a week and would like to live with the grandparents.

The least contact was with the biological father; only one child had this contact. A telephone contact was initiated by the father, not the child. Although the contact was not disruptive, the adoptive parent indicated that the child felt "no common ground with the father." In 1 other case the father would like to have contact, but the adoptive parents prevent direct contact. One additional case mentions the father, but this is in reference to the fact that abuse issues involving the father prevent contact with a half-sibling who still resides with the father.

For the most part, the effects of these contacts were evaluated positively. Over time the number of parents who reported that it was "mostly bad" decreased, suggesting that over time the influences were evaluated as less negative. Table 3.3 presents results about contacts with the biological family.

Results suggest that a significant percent of children have contact with the biological family and that this contact, for the most part, has a positive effect on the child and the adoptive family.

ATTACHMENT ISSUES

Attachment was examined from two different theoretical perspectives (see Chapter 2). One perspective includes the dimensions of communication, trust, getting along, respect, and closeness. The other perspective grows out of the ethological theory and research and examines patterns of avoidant and anxious attachment.

Figure 3.1 presents data on various aspects of parent/child relationships over time. The results were initially analyzed by gender, and there were no significant differences between males and females. Over time, there is a statistically significant decrease in how positively the parent/child relationship is perceived; that is, relations become more negative. However, even with the decrease, most parents reported they and their spouses have very positive relations with their adopted children. During all 4 years, about 90% of parents reported that they and their spouses got along fairly to very well with their adopted children. Communication with the children was rated as good or excellent for almost 80% in all 4 years. Trust changed the most dramatically. In year 1, only 9% indicated that they did not trust their children; by year 4, this increased to 19%. Still, themajority of families were positive about trusting their children. Over 80% of the families each year reported that they felt close to their children. Thus, even though there was a trend to less positive parent/child relations over time, relations remained quite good.

Another way to examine attachment develops from the work of Bowlby and colleagues (Bowlby, 1969, 1973, 1988; Ainsworth, 1973; Main, Kaplan, & Cassidy, 1985; Main & Weston, 1981). Difficulties in attachment develop when caregivers are unresponsive, unavailable, rejecting, or hurtful in meeting the needs of the children. Attachment difficulties have been classified into two main topologies: anxious or avoidant (Ainsworth, 1973; Bowlby, 1988). Main and Weston (1981) suggest children who have been maltreated blend both avoidant and anxious attachment behaviors, so no attempt was made in this study to find mutually exclusive patterns. The measures for these attachment patterns are described elsewhere (Groze & Rosenthal, 1993).

Figure 3.2 presents results for the 4 years for both anxious and avoidant patterns of attachment. No trends are statistically significant. This suggests that patterns of avoidant and anxious attachment do not significantly change over time.

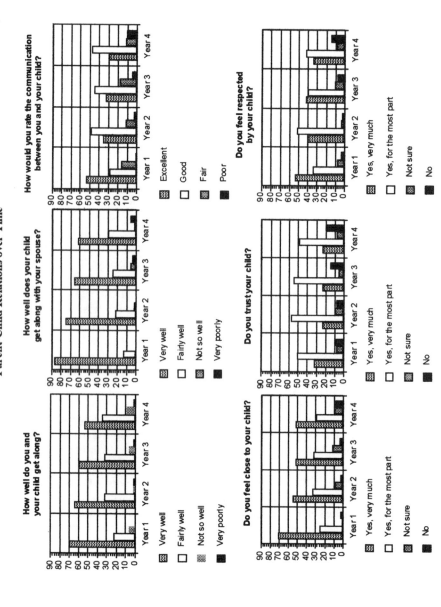

Figure 3.1
Parent-Child Relations over Time

Figure 3.2
Patterns of Attachment over Time

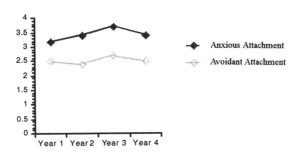

CHILDREN'S BEHAVIOR

Ratings of children's behaviors were obtained by the Child Behavior Checklist (CBC) developed by Achenbach and Edelbrock (1983). The portion of the CBC used in this research was the list of 113 behavior problems; items were scored with the 1991 calculations for the CBC (Achenbach, 1991).

When raw scores are examined, several trends are notable. Regarding internalizing problems, there is a linear trend that approaches significance for anxiety and depression (p=.07). Over time, there is an increase in anxiety and depression for all the children. In addition, there is a difference between boys and girls in thought problems that approaches significance (p=.06), with boys evidencing more thought difficulties than girls. Regarding externalizing behaviors, there are increases in attention problems, delinquent behavior, and total problems. There are also some significant gender differences, with boys evidencing more attention problems and more total problems.

Raw score results are not the best indicator of behavior changes. As children get older, there is a change in many behaviors. One way to account for the effects of age and an additional way to examine behavior over time is to compare scores to some norms that have been developed. Since the norms are developed according to gender and age groups, comparison scores were computed by subtracting the raw scores found in this study from the normative score for each gender (male and female) and age grouping (4 to 11 and 12 to 18). For example, in year 1 the score for each boy who was 4 to 11 years old was subtracted from the mean score for boys 4 to 11 referred for mental health services as presented by Achenbach (1991, p. 252). The same process was followed for each study year, in the appropriate gender and age group, and for nonclinical norms. Results are interpreted that if the mean is positive, then the average score for the adoption group was above the average score for the children referred for mental health services (i.e., the clinical group). Conversely, if the mean is negative, then the average score for the adoption group was below the average score for the children referred for mental health services. The closer the mean scores are to zero, the more similar are the mean scores to the scores for the normative group.

Table 3.4 presents the mean difference scores between ratings of internalizing problems for the study's boys and girls compared to the means for clinical (referred) and nonclinical (nonreferred) children. In general, mean scores are below the clinical group and above the nonclinical group, and several trends are statistically significant. Over the 4 years, the mean scores for anxiety and depression for boys become similar to scores for the clinical group. This trend is similar to the raw score trend reported earlier.

Table 3.5 presents the mean difference scores between ratings of externalizing problems for this study's boys and girls compared to the means for clinical and nonclinical children. Several trends are statistically significant. In general, mean scores for both boys and girls are higher than mean scores for the nonreferred or nonclinical children. Over the 4 years, the mean scores for attention problems for boys increased and are slightly higher than the mean scores for the clinical group. This trend is similar for delinquent and aggressive behavior for boys, although it does not reach statistical significance. Mean scores for total problem and externalizing scales, while below the mean compared to referred children, significantly increase over time for boys. This suggests that by the fourth year, boys score similarly on these scales to boys being referred for mental health services.

Overall, results suggest that the adopted children continue to experience behavior problems. The behavioral ratings show that a significant percent of adopted children evidence behavioral difficulties in some areas during all 4 years, a finding supported by previous cross-sectional research (Berry & Barth, 1989; Rosenthal & Groze, 1991) and a preliminary analysis of the data during the second year (Groze, in press).

FAMILY FUNCTIONING

To assess family functioning, the Family Adaptability and Cohesion Evaluation Scales (FACES III) were used.[3] FACES provides information about two dimensions of family functioning: cohesion and adaptability. Family cohesion is the feelings of

---

3. Subsequent to the study, psychometric difficulties with FACES III resulted in the authors of FACES III suggesting that FACES II be employed. However, there were methodological difficulties with changing instruments after the second year, so the same instrument was used throughout the 4 years of the study.

Table 3.4
Repeated Measures Analysis of Variance (MANOVA) on the Child Behavior Checklist Comparing Mean Scores of Adoption Sample to a Normative "Clinical" Group and "Nonclinical" Group for Internalizing Problems

	Clinical Scores		Nonclinical Scores	
	Boys	Girls	Boys	Girls
INTERNALIZING PROBLEMS				
Withdrawal				
Year 1	-1.6	-2.6	.8	.3
Year 2	-1.9	-2.4	.6	.6
Year 3	-1.9	-2.1	.7	.9
Year 4	-1.4	-2.6	1.2	.5
Somatic Complaints				
Year 1	-.6	-.6	.4	2.1
Year 2	-.4	-.5	.7	2.6
Year 3	-.5	-.0	.5	2.7
Year 4	-.6	-.3	.4	2.4
Anxiety/Depression				
Year 1	-4.3	-3.1	.4	2.1
Year 2	-3.8	-2.6	.9	2.6
Year 3	-3.0	-2.5	1.7	2.7
Year 4	-2.2*	-2.8	2.4*	2.4
Social Problems				
Year 1	-.7	-.6	2.0	2.1
Year 2	.4	.2	3.0	2.7
Year 3	-.1	.1	2.5	2.6
Year 4	.1	-.3	2.7	2.1
Thought Problems				
Year 1	-.3	-.8	1.1	.6
Year 2	.1	-.7	1.5	.7
Year 3	-.2	-.5	1.2	1.0
Year 4	.3	-.6	1.8	.8
Internalizing Scale				
Year 1	-6.2	-6.4	1.4	2.4
Year 2	-6.0	-5.8	1.8	3.2
Year 3	-5.4	-4.5	2.3	4.5
Year 4	-4.2	-6.6	3.6	2.6

*linear trend, p<.05

Note: The clinical group are children referred for mental health services, and the nonclinical group are children not referred for mental health services, as presented in Appendix B by Achenbach (1991).

Table 3.5
Repeated MANOVA on the Child Behavior
Checklist Comparing Mean Scores of Adoption Sample
to a "Clinical" Group and "Nonclinical" Group
for Externalizing Problems

	Clinical Scores		Nonclinical Scores	
	Boys	Girls	Boys	Girls
EXTERNALIZING PROBLEMS				
Attention Problems				
Year 1	-1.8	-1.4	3.1	3.3
Year 2	.3	-1.4	5.2	3.3
Year 3	.1	-.7	5.0	3.9
Year 4	.1*	-1.5	5.1*	3.1
Delinquent Behavior				
Year 1	-1.0	-1.0	2.0	1.9
Year 2	-1.1	-1.0	2.2	2.2
Year 3	-.3	-.3	3.1	3.0
Year 4	.3#	-1.0	3.8*	2.4
Aggressive Behavior				
Year 1	-3.9	-2.3	4.2	4.8
Year 2	-2.8	-1.8	5.1	5.3
Year 3	-1.6	-.7	6.3	6.3
Year 4	-.8#	-1.5	7.0#	5.5
Externalizing Scale				
Year 1	-4.9	-3.2	6.2	6.8
Year 2	-3.9	-2.8	7.3	7.5
Year 3	-1.8	-1.0	9.4	9.3
Year 4	-.5*	-2.5	10.8*	7.9
Total Problems				
Year 1	-15.2	-11.8	14.9	17.8
Year 2	-10.2	-11.5	19.7	18.3
Year 3	-7.5	-8.3	22.4	21.5
Year 4	-3.7*	-11.6	26.2	18.4

*linear trend, $p < .05$
#linear trend, approaches significance, $p < .10$

Note: The clinical group are children referred for mental health services, and the nonclinical group are children not referred for mental health services, as presented in Appendix B by Achenbach (1991).

closeness that family members have toward one another. Family adaptability is the ability of a family system to change in response to situational and developmental stress.

Mean scores over time and the norms provided by Olson are provided in Table 3.6. Over the 4-year period, there is a statistically significant decrease in mean adaptability scores. Even with the decrease, mean scores for the four years are higher

Table 3.6
Assessment of Family Functioning over Time

Family Adaptability

	Year 1	Year 2	Year 3	Year 4	Olson's Norms for All Families	Olson's Norms for Families with Adolescents
Mean	26.3	24.8	25.1	24.7*	24.1	24.3
SD	4.6	5.5	6.3	5.2	4.7	4.8

Family Cohesion

	Year 1	Year 2	Year 3	Year 4	Olson's Norms for All Families	Olson's Norms for Families with Adolescents
Mean	41.6	39.7	39.2	39.8*	39.8	37.1
SD	4.6	6.7	6.5	6.0	5.4	6.1

*$p < .05$, linear trend

than the norms provided by Olson. In addition, by the fourth year, when most of the children are in adolescence, the mean score is higher than Olson's norms for family adaptability in families with adolescents.

There is also a statistically significant decrease over time in mean cohesion scores. However, by the fourth year, when most of the children are in adolescence, the mean cohesion score is the same as Olson's norms for all families and higher than the mean for Olson's norms for families with adolescents. These results suggest that, even though there is a decrease in adaptability and cohesion over time, families remain more adaptable and cohesive than normative families. This supports previous cross-sectional research (Groze & Rosenthal, 1991a) and theory (Rosenberg, 1992) that suggested that the life cycle sequence of adoptive families is different from the life cycle of biological families.

In addition to examining mean scores, the Olson family functioning scores can be categorized. The categories of adaptability are chaotic, flexible, structured, and rigid. The categories of cohesion are disengaged, separated, connected, and enmeshed. Figure 3.3 graphs the percent of families scoring in each category over the 4 years and the proportion in each category for the normative group developed by Olson.

The results suggest that during all 4 years, a greater percent of adoptive families were chaotic than the normative families described by Olson and colleagues. In addition, very few families' scores are rigid during the first year compared to scores of normative families. Initially, adoptive families with special needs children were more adaptable than normative families. As offered in a previous cross-sectional analysis of family functioning (Groze & Rosenthal, 1991a), flexibility facilitates integration of the child into the family system. Flexibility allows families to tolerate a

Figure 3.3
Categories of Adaptability and Cohesion over Time
and Compared to Normative Data

Adaptability

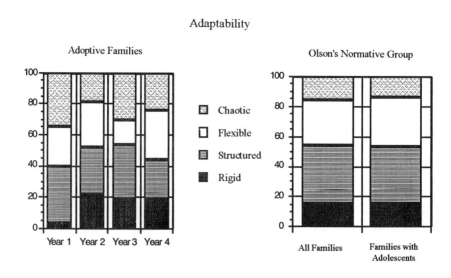

Cohesiveness

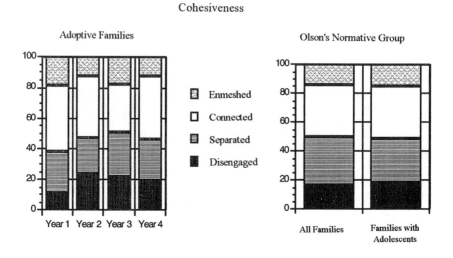

wider range of difficult behavior in children entering the family system. However, in subsequent years there was a marked increase in the percent of families scoring at a rigid level of adaptability. Overall, families begin to approximate the norms on the proportion who are structured or rigid.

The picture for family cohesiveness is less clear. Initially, a greater percent of families were connected or enmeshed compared to normative families. Over time, the percent of families in each category approximates those percents for normative families. Initially, the special needs adoptive families demonstrated close relationships among family members. This was a family system reaction that may have been in response to the child's psychosocial immaturity, the child's desire to compensate for the lack of close parental ties in previous settings, or the need to integrate the child into the family system before beginning the task of separation (Groze & Rosenthal, 1991). Over time, as these tasks are resolved, there is a movement away from cohesiveness. In addition, one way that families successfully manage continual behavioral problems is to emotionally distance themselves from the problems. This emotional distancing allows them to separate themselves from the problems while at the same time maintaining the child in the home.

Another way to interpret the results is to view the changes as a result of the bonding process. Initially, the emphasis on bonding is for family members to be close to each other and to build a relationship. Most of these children and their families have an extensive history apart from each other before joining as a new family. At the onset of the relationship, much effort is spent on building a relationship. Over time, once there is some resolution on the level of closeness between parent(s) and child, the children and parents begin to separate. In addition, in the normal course of the life cycle, parents and children will be quite close initially, and, as children begin to enter adolescence, they will begin to distance themselves from the family.

As a final analysis of family functioning, individual items assessing family cohesion and adaptability were examined over time. Table 3.7 presents individual components of family cohesion, and Table 3.8 presents individual items for family adaptability. Several changes are remarkable. Among the cohesion items, there is a significant tendency over time for families to decrease in their approval of each other's friends and to decrease family activities oriented just toward the family. Of course, this is consistent with what is expected in families as children get older. Also, over time, families become less flexible in shifting household chores and less flexible in including children in decision making.

It appears from the analysis of subscale items that the changes that are occurring in adoptive families may reflect the life cycle changes that would normally be expected of families with adolescents.

ADOPTION OUTCOMES

Several different indicators of adoption outcomes were assessed. During all 4

Table 3.7
Repeated MANOVA for Individual Items Assessing Family Cohesion

Scoring: 1 =   Almost never
            2 =   Once in a while
            3 =   Sometimes
            4 =   Frequently
            5 =   Almost always

Cohesion Items	Year 1	Year 2	Year 3	Year 4
Family members ask each other for help.				
Mean				
(Standard Deviation)	4.0	3.9	3.9	3.9
	(.83)	(.79)	(1.0)	(.89)
We approve of each other's friends.				
Mean	4.5	4.0	4.1	3.9*
(Standard Deviation)	(.69)	(.91)	(.99)	(.97)
We like to do things with just the immediate family.				
Mean	3.9	3.7	3.7	3.6*
(Standard Deviation)	(.75)	(.77)	(.93)	(.71)
Family members feel closer to other family members than to people outside the family.				
Mean				
(Standard Deviation)	4.3	4.1	4.1	4.2
	(.95)	(1.1)	(1.1)	(1.1)
Family members like to spend free time with each other.				
Mean	4.0	3.8	3.8	3.8#
(Standard Deviation)	(.75)	(.80)	(.87)	(.82)
Family members feel very close to each other.				
Mean	4.3	4.3	4.1	4.2#
(Standard Deviation)	(.84)	(.88)	(1.1)	(.99)

Table 3.7 (Continued)

When our family gets together for activities,
everybody is present.

Mean	4.0	4.0	3.8	3.8
(Standard Deviation)	(1.0)	(.97)	(1.2)	(.96)

We can easily think of things to do together
as a family.

Mean	4.2	4.2	3.9	4.2*
(Standard Deviation)	(.86)	(.95)	(1.1)	(.90)

Family members consult other family
members on their decisions.

Mean	3.7	3.7	3.7	3.6
(Standard Deviation)	(.99)	(1.0)	(.93)	(1.2)

Family togetherness is important.

Mean	4.6	4.4	4.3	4.5*
(Standard Deviation)	(.58)	(.75)	(.83)	(.73)

* $p<.05$, # $p<.10$

years, parents were asked about the smoothness of the adoption and the impact of the adoption on the family. During the last year, families were asked how often they thought of ending the adoptive placement. Also, at the last point of data collection and as suggested by Pinderhughes and Talen (1993, personal communication), families were asked whether they would adopt again and would recommend adoption to others. Table 3.9 presents data on adoption outcomes collected for all 4 years and those items collected during the fourth year.

Over the 4 years, there are some significant shifts. Whereas during the first year about 30% of families thought the adoption had more ups and downs than they expected, by the fourth year this had increased to 42%. Likewise, while about 78% of respondents reported the adoption impact to be mostly or very positive, by the fourth year 69% still felt the same way. While the majority were still very positive, there was some shift to less positive perceptions of these outcomes. Nevertheless, most families (over 90%) have not thought of ending the adoptive placement and would themselves adopt again. Although about 40% agreed mildly or strongly that they would advise others not to adopt, over 60% had a favorable response to recommending adoption to others. Thus, while results are somewhat less positive over time, overall, families remain quite positive about the adoption, and outcomes remain quite good.

Table 3.8
Repeated MANOVA for Individual Items Assessing Family Adaptability

Scoring: 1 =   Almost never
            2 =   Once in a while
            3 =   Sometimes
            4 =   Frequently
            5 =   Almost always

Adaptability Items	Year 1	Year 2	Year 3	Year 4
In solving problems, the children's suggestions are followed.				
Mean	3.1	2.9	3.0	3.0
(Standard Deviation)	(.75)	(.65)	(.90)	(.67)
Children have a say in their discipline.				
Mean	3.0	2.9	2.8	2.8
(Standard Deviation)	(.84)	(.87)	(1.0)	(.95)
Different persons act as leaders in our family.				
Mean	2.7	2.5	2.4	2.3
(Standard Deviation)	(1.2)	(1.1)	(1.2)	(1.1)
Our family changes its way of handling tasks.				
Mean	2.9	3.1	3.0	2.8
(Standard Deviation)	(.92)	(.90)	(1.0)	(.81)
Parents and children discuss punishment together.				
Mean	3.8	3.3	3.3	3.3
(Standard Deviation)	(1.0)	(1.1)	(1.1)	(1.2)*
The children make the decisions in our family.				
Mean	2.0	1.7	1.7	1.8*
(Standard Deviation)	(.88)	(.78)	(.90)	(.75)

Table 3.8 (Continued)

Rules change in our family.				
Mean	2.3	2.2	2.3	2.2
(Standard Deviation)	(.85)	(.92)	(.98)	(.85)

We shift household responsibilities from person to person.				
Mean	3.4	2.9	3.1	3.0*
(Standard Deviation)	(1.1)	(1.1)	(1.1)	(1.1)

It is hard to identify the leader(s) in our family.				
Mean	1.5	1.8	1.6	1.6
(Standard Deviation)	(.94)	(1.1)	(.97)	(.95)

It is hard to tell who does which household chores.				
Mean	1.8	1.8	2.0	2.0
(Standard Deviation)	(1.0)	(.94)	(1.2)	(1.0)

* $p<.05$

Adoption outcomes over time were examined by the different special needs of the children. However, neither physical disabilities nor mental retardation affects adoption outcomes over time. There are some differences in adoption impact on the family with age at placement. More negative impact for children placed over the age of 5 was found compared to children placed younger, although there is no trend over time. That is, the adoption's impact over time does not get more negative for children placed when older compared to children placed at a younger age. The smoothness of the adoption is unrelated to age at placement, and placement age does not affect parent perception of smoothness over time.

Several of the indicators of adoption outcomes were categorical variables. These variables were recoded into dichotomies. For the question, "I would advise others not to adopt," responses were coded so that those who strongly disagree were in one category (advise, N=40), and all other responses were coded into the second category (not advise, N=31). For the question, "I would adopt again," responses were coded so that those who reported they strongly agree were in one category (N=54) and all other responses were in the other category (N=17). Discriminant analysis was conducted to determine if it is possible to differentiate between categories of responses.

Discriminant analysis is a multivariate technique, analogous to multiple regression, used when the dependent variable or criterion variable is categorical, and the independent variables or predictor variables are continuous (Betz, 1987; Klecka,

Table 3.9
Ratings of Adoption Outcomes over 4 Years

Overall impact of the adoption on the family	Year 1	Year 2	Year 3	Year 4
Very positive	51.6	40.6	42.2	39.1
Mostly positive	26.6	37.5	34.4	29.7
Mixed	18.8	15.6	17.2	18.8
Mostly negative	3.1	6.3	3.1	12.5
Very negative			3.1	1.6
Overall smoothness of adoption				
Smoother than expected	24.6	27.5	18.8	20.3
About as expected	44.9	39.1	44.9	37.7
More ups & downs	30.4	33.3	36.2	42.0

Adoption Outcomes Assessed During Fourth Year

How often do you think of ending the
adoption placement?
Never	78.3% (47)
Not very often	15.0% (9)
Most of the time	1.7% (1)
Frequently	5.0% (3)

I would adopt again
Strongly agree	84.4% (54)
Mildly agree	6.3% (4)
Mildly disagree	3.1% (2)
Strongly disagree	6.3% (4)

I would advise others not to adopt
Strongly disagree	50.0% (33)
Mildly disagree	10.6% (7)
Mildly agree	19.7% (13)
Strongly agree	19.7% (13)

1980). Discriminant analysis can be used to classify cases; that is, a prediction of group membership can be made for each individual in the sample and compared to actual group membership. In this study, that means those predicted to advise others not to adopt can be compared to those who actually would advise others not to adopt, and those predicted to indicate they would adopt again can be compared to those reported they would adopt again. The actual percentage of correct predictions can be compared statistically to the expected prediction based on chance by using the Z test for the difference of proportions (Blalock, 1979; Glass & Stanley, 1970; Betz, 1987). A backward elimination stepwise variable selection was employed, similar to the procedure used in the regression analysis (see Tables 3.10 and 3.11).

Table 3.10
Discriminant Analysis of Advice to Others to Adopt: Reduced Model

	Standardized Canonical Discriminant Function Coefficient
Advice to others considering adoption	
Change in Family Adaptability	-.4503
Change in Parent-Child Communication	.5842
Change in Respect from Child	.3642
Total Number of Handicaps	-.4856
Length of Time in Adoptive Home	.6061
Change in Income	.3869

	Predicted Group		
Actual Group	**Not Advise**	**Advise**	**Total**
Not Advise			
n	12	11	23
%	52.2%	47.8%	41.1%
Advise			
n	6	27	33
%	18.2%	81.8%	58.9%
Total			
n	18	38	56
%	32.1%	67.9%	

Percent of "grouped" cases correctly classified: 69.6%
Percent of cases correctly classified by chance: 53.2%[2]
$[(41.1)(32.1) + (58.9)(67.9)]$

$Z^3 = 1.80$, p = ns

For the question asking about advising others about adoption, change in family adaptability, change in some elements of the attachment relationship, change in income, the total number of handicaps, and the length of time in the home are significantly associated with responses. Using these variables, 70% of the cases were correctly classified. Fifty-two percent of respondents who would not advise others to adopt and 82% of respondents who would advise others to adopt were correctly classified. This suggests that these variables are useful in predicting which parents would advise and not advise others about adoption. For the question asking about whether the respondent would adopt again, change in family cohesion, change in some elements of the attachment relationship, age at placement, and sexual abuse history are significantly associated with responses.

Table 3.11
Discriminant Analysis of Adopting Again: Reduced Model

	Standardized Canonical Discriminant Function Coefficient
I would adopt again	
Change in Family Cohesion	.3781
Change in Anxious Attachment	-.2692
Change in Parent-Child Communication	.3411
Age at Placement	-.8378
Known or Suspected Sexual Abuse	.7897

	Predicted Group		
Actual Group	**Other**	**Strongly Agree**	**Total**
Other			
n	7	2	9
%	77.8%	22.2%	17.0%
Strongly Agree			
n	9	35	44
%	20.5%	79.5%	83.0%
Total			
n	16	37	53
%	30.2%	69.8%	

Percent of "grouped" cases correctly classified:	79.3%
Percent of cases correctly classified by chance:	63.1%
$[(17.0)(30.2) + (83.0)(69.8)]$	

$Z = 1.79$, p = ns

Using these variables, 79% of the cases were correctly classified. About 80% of respondents who would adopt again and 78% of respondents who responded otherwise were correctly classified. This suggests that these variables are useful in predicting which parents would adopt again and not adopt again. In addition, the standardized canonical discriminant function coefficients can be interpreted in a similar manner to beta weights, giving an indication of the strength of each variable in the model.

UNDERSTANDING CHANGES

The next series of analysis were conducted to examine predictors of change. First, changes in attachment patterns are probed. Next, factors affecting changes in total behavior problems, internalizing problems, and externalizing problems are examined. Third, changes in family adaptability and cohesion are analyzed. Finally, factors affecting changes in adoption impact are explored.

To explore changes, a regression analysis is conducted of change scores. The computation of change scores is explained in each section, as well as the variables used in each analysis. A forward method is used in the regression model. With the forward method, variables are entered into the equation one at a time. At each step in the equation, the independent variables not in the equation are examined for entry.

Changes in Patterns of Attachment

The parents' evaluation of the different measure of attachment during the first year was subtracted from parents' evaluation during the fourth year to obtain change scores. For anxious attachment, between the fourth and first years about 33% of the children decreased this pattern, 30% remained the same, and 38% increased anxious attachment behavior. For avoidant attachment, between the fourth and first years about 31% of the children decreased this pattern, 34% remained the same, and 34% increased anxious attachment behavior. For feeling close, between the fourth and first years about 35% of the parents reported a decrease, 56% remained the same, and 9% reported increased closeness. For getting along, between the fourth and first years about 30% of the parents reported a decrease, 63% remained the same, and 8% increased getting along. For feeling respected by the child, between the fourth and first years about 38% of the parents reported a decrease, 54% remained the same, and 7% increased respect. For communication between the parent and the child, between the fourth and first years about 40% of the parents reported a decrease, 54% remained the same, and 6% increased communication.

Each attachment variable was analyzed separately. Changes in child's behavior, changes in family functioning, and changes in family income, as well as the age of placement, the length of time in the home, the age of the child during the fourth year, and the gender of the child (coded as a dummy variable), were included in regression equations to examine the relationship of these variables to each of the attachment variables.

The regression equations predicting changes in avoidant and anxious attachment were not statistically significant. This suggests that these independent variables were not good predictors of changes in these patterns. The regression equation predicting changes in getting along was statistically significant ($F=5.50$, $p<.01$), explaining 14% of the variance in changes in getting along. The length of time in the home ($b=.44$) and the age of the child at year 4 ($b=-.32$) were statistically significant effects in the equation. This can be interpreted that, as the length of time in the home increases, there is an increase in getting along. At the same time, as age increases, there is a decrease in getting along. The remainder of the coefficients in the following regression equations are not stated but follow the same interpretation.

The regression equation predicting changes in feeling close was statistically significant (F=6.90, p<.01), explaining 17% of the variance in changes in feeling close. Change in family cohesion (b=.28) and changes in family adaptability (b=-.28) were statistically significant effects in the equation.

The regression equation predicting changes in respect was statistically significant (F=5.79, p=.02), explaining 8% of the variance in changes in respect. Change in family cohesion (b=.31) was the only statistically significant effect in the equation.

The regression equation predicting changes in communicating was statistically significant (F=4.57, p=.04), explaining 6% of the variance in changes in communicating. Change in income (b=-.28) was the only statistically significant effect in the equation.

The regression equation predicting changes in trust was statistically significant (F=5.27, p=.03), explaining 7% of the variance in changes in trust. Change in family cohesion (b=.30) was the only statistically significant effect in the equation.

For the most part, a modest amount of variance in changes in attachment is explained by these variables. This suggests that other variables not included in the equation predict a greater proportion of changes in attachment patterns. In addition, there was no consistency in the variable(s) that predict changes. This supports the assertion that attachment is a multidimensional concept. However, the explanatory power of the variables included in the analyses is low.

Changes in Behavior

First-year scores on the internalizing, externalizing and total problem scales from the CBC were subtracted from the fourth-year scores to obtain change scores. For internalizing behaviors, between the fourth and first years about 37% of the children decreased internalizing behaviors, 9% remained the same, and 55% increased internalizing behaviors. For externalizing behaviors, between the fourth and first years about 34% of the children decreased externalizing behaviors, 11% remained the same, and 55% increased externalizing behaviors. For total behavior problems, between the fourth and first years about 38% of the children decreased total problems, 7% remained the same, and 55% increased total problems. Changes in family functioning and changes in family income, as well as the age of placement, the length of time in the home, the age of the child during the fourth year, and the gender of the child, were included in regression equations to examine the relationship of these variables in each of the behavior subscales. The attachment variables were highly correlated with each other and the behavior scales, so they were excluded in this analysis. The regression equations for changes in internalizing problems, externalizing problems, and total problems were not statistically significant. This suggests that these variables are not good predictors of changes in these behavior scores.

Changes in Family Functioning

Scores for family adaptability and family cohesion from the first year were subtracted from fourth-year scores to obtain change scores. For family adaptability, between the fourth and first years about 59% of the families reported a decrease in adaptability, 14% remained the same, and 28% increased adaptability. For family cohesion, between the fourth and first years about 61% of the families reported a decrease in cohesion, 9% remained the same, and 30% increased cohesion. Changes in child's behavior, changes in the different components of attachment, changes in family income, the age at placement, the length of time in the home, the age of the child during the fourth year, and the gender of the child were included in regression equations to examine the relationship of these variables in each of the dimensions of family functioning.

The regression equations predicting changes in adaptability was not statistically significant. The regression equation predicting changes in family cohesion that includes only change in closeness (b=.39) is statistically significant (F=8.38, p<.01), explaining 13% of the variance in change in family cohesion.

Changes in Adoption Outcomes

A regression analysis was conducted to examine what factors affect changes in adoption impact. The parents' evaluation of adoption impact in the first year was subtracted from their evaluation in the fourth year. For adoption impact, between the fourth and first years about 10% of the families reported a decrease in impact, 59% remained the same, and 31% increased impact. Variables assessing changes in child behavior, changes in family functioning, changes in family income, and changes in attachment, as well as age at year 4, age at placement, length of time in home, and gender, were included.

The regression equation predicting changes in adoption impact was statistically significant (F=13.2, p=<.01), explaining 50% of the variance in changes in adoption impact. Results suggests that changes in family adaptability (b=.30), changes in communication (b=-.36), changes in respect (b=-.38), and changes in family income (-.24) significantly affect changes in adoption impact. This can be interpreted that as income increased, adoption impact decreased (i.e., became more negative). Likewise, as communication and respect decreased, adoption impact increased. Finally, as family adaptability increased, adoption impact increased.

SUMMARY OF MAJOR FINDINGS

These adoptive placements were very stable during the 4 years, with very few children ending up out of the home. Referring back to the resources and stressors outlined in Chapter 1, there were significant challenges and assets to meet the challenges. School was a resource for most families, with many children enjoying school and performing well. Learning problems, which could have been a stressor, were mediated by involvement with special education programs. Several parents commented on how the special education programs in their school district helped their child be successful in school. Contact with the child's biological family was not a stressor to most family systems. In fact, these contacts were generally evaluated positively, and the families became more positive about these contacts over time.

There was a decrease in parent/child relations over time, a finding that is consistent with the life cycle changes observed in parent/child relations in biological families. Even with the decrease in parent/child relations, attachment itself remained quite positive for the majority of families in all 4 years. In addition, the different components of the attachment relationship (getting along, feeling respected, feeling close, and communication) remained the same for most children. The positive attachments and consistently positive attachments between the parent and adopted child were a resource for the families. Families continued to feel positive about their children. Most of the variables studied did not explain many of the changes that occurred in the different ways of measuring attachment.

A significant stressor was the child's behavior. The children demonstrated significant behavior difficulties. In addition, some behavior difficulties became more pronounced over time. Over half the families report an increase in internalizing behaviors, externalizing behaviors, and total problems between the first and fourth years of the study. Families particularly struggled with children's anxiety, depression, attention difficulties, and aggressive behavior.

Family functioning changed over the 4 years, with family adaptability and cohesion decreasing. However, in the fourth year, families were still more flexible and closer than what would be expected of biological families at the same point in their life cycle. Thus, adaptability and cohesion were additional resources to these families.

Finally, there was a slight tendency for the impact of the adoption and other adoption outcomes to be less positive over time. However, even with the trend to less positive outcomes, outcomes were still very positive, and parent evaluation of adoption impact did not change between the first and fourth years for the majority of families. Results for all 3 measures of adoption outcomes suggest that family system variables such as adaptability, cohesion, and elements of the attachment relationship have an effect on parents' evaluation of outcomes. These are critical issues to pay attention to, both in preparing families for adoption and in assisting families when difficulties arise.

Overall, these results provide support for many of the conclusions provided by previous cross-sectional studies. The findings also help to begin to develop a better understanding of the issues faced by families of special needs adoptees over time. Adoptive family life was marked by accomplishments and triumphs as well as trials and tribulations. Several parents throughout the four years worried about the future of their children, particularly their ability to obtain gainful employment and live independently. Although a special needs adoption at times was a mixed blessing, it is a choice that the vast majority of these families would make again, and would recommend to others, and a choice in which they found enjoyment and rewards.

While the results presented in this chapter give an overall view of changes over the 4 years, the next few chapters examine specific adoption issues in more detail. The following chapter examines adoption outcomes and issues for siblings placed together and apart. Some of the same issues reviewed are examined but in the context of sibling relations.

4

Siblings Placed Together and Apart

INTRODUCTION

Most children grow up with siblings. In the child population in the United States, it is estimated that more than 80% of children belong to a sibling group, and 60% have at least two siblings. The time siblings spend together in their early years is often greater than the time they spend with their parents. The sibling relationship is complex and lasts for a lifetime, longer than most marriages and parent/child relationships (Pfouts, 1976; Dunn, 1985).

Sibling relations exert considerable influence on individual development and attachment behavior in each other, particularly in the early childhood and adolescent years (Bank & Kahn, 1982; Pfouts, 1976; Sutton-Smith, 1982; LePere, Davis, Couve, & McDonald, 1986). Sutton-Smith (1982) and LePere et al. (1986) suggest that sibling relations assist children in developing a private identity and a public identity. Within the family, children teach each other the values and norms of the family. From sibling relations, children learn, in part, how to make and maintain intimate relationships. For example, when children show concern over the anxiety of a sibling and attempt to alleviate this stress through getting a favorite toy or talking to the sibling, this suggests an understanding of the other's feelings and ideas about how to comfort the other. Through these interactions children learn about particular feelings, intentions, and needs of persons other than themselves and the social rules of the family in which they are growing up (Dunn, 1985). These skills influence the development of the individual's personality and social behavior. Outside the family, children also often provide cues to each other about what is acceptable and unacceptable public behavior. They help each other differentiate between the behaviors and ideas that may be expressed in the intimacy of the immediate family and those that can be shared with others outside the family.

The author would like to gratefully acknowledge Kelly Corcoran-Rumppe, whose thesis work provided background for this chapter, and Jane Sibley for her assistance with the qualitative data.

During the early school years, siblings spend time together in imitative activities. They also may indirectly influence which children take on different family roles. As siblings grow up, their different talents and abilities become increasingly apparent. These differences contribute to their being "assigned" different roles. For example, as the first child reaches middle childhood, she or he may have more responsibilities for the younger child(ren) and, therefore, take on the role of caretaking child. The roles that an individual is given within his or her family has an impact on his or her individual development, particularly in the area of self-esteem (Dunn, 1985).

Siblings also influence attachment behavior in each other. For example, older siblings are often supplemental attachment figures and caregivers for younger siblings. Common situations in which this relationship could occur include when the older child recognizes some danger to the younger sibling, in a cooperative family system where the older sibling is asked to help or relieve the parent in caregiving while the parent is doing another task, and in family systems where the adults are unable or unwilling to carry out the parental role appropriately (Dunn, 1985; Hegar, 1988; Smith & Howard, 1991). Even in healthy large families it is not unusual for older children to provide love, support, nurturance, and guidance to younger siblings. Stewart and Marvin (1984) indicate that, by the end of preschool years, children are able to serve as subsidiary attachment and caregiving figures for their younger siblings.

Sibling relations are not without conflict. It is not unusual for there to be conflict or rivalry at different stages in the relationship between siblings. However, rivalry and conflict are not necessarily negative. Bank and Kahn (1982) suggest that sibling rivalry, particularly aggression, offers individuals the opportunity to learn flexibility, play, competence, and a good sense of fair play. These skills are used in relationships with family and peers and, as adults, with spouses or significant other relationships. According to Dunn (1983), arguments also assist in the development of attitudes toward social rules and the growth of argument skills. Discussions and arguments between siblings provide an opportunity to resolve conflicts without the aid of an adult, to learn to understand the perspective of the other sibling, and to develop an understanding of the purpose of social rules.

It is unclear how much sibling relationships affect adult personality. Nevertheless, the power of the relationship lasts far past childhood (Cicirelli, 1982; Hegar, 1988), withstands separations of time and space, and provides emotional strength for most people in later life stages. Contact with siblings in late adulthood provides a sense of nearness, belonging, and the assurance of attachment to a family. It provides a shield against the insecurity of aging and the loss of parents (Dunn, 1985; Hegar, 1988).

With a recognition of the critical role sibling relations play, it is dismal that little research has been conducted on siblings in the child welfare system. There are ample anecdotes and rhetoric about the value of sibling relations but few empirical studies.

SIBLINGS AND THE CHILD WELFARE SYSTEM

A critical issue in child welfare is siblings in care. Studies suggest that of children in foster care, 93% had full, half-, or stepsiblings (Timberlake & Hamlin, 1982) and 30% to 85% of children enter foster care with a sibling (Wedge & Mantle, 1991).

Foster and adoption workers are often faced with the question of whether it is better to place siblings together or whether it is better to split them up. Once the decision is made to separate siblings, then the issue becomes whether to place siblings individually or in subgroups when looking for foster or adoptive family placements. Factors affecting placement decisions regarding siblings include worker and agency philosophy (Jones & Niblett, 1985; Ward, 1984), sibling interaction (Ward, 1984), circumstances of the child when entering the child welfare system (Ward, 1984; Wedge & Mantle, 1991), and placement availability (Ward, 1984; Jones & Niblett, 1985).

Perhaps the single most significant factor affecting placement decisions is how siblings enter the child welfare system. Many agencies endorse a policy of keeping children together. While an agency might be philosophically committed to sibling placements, individual workers who become the "gatekeepers" of placement often have difficulty locating a placement for any child. In addition, the worker's own personal values have considerable impact on professional decisions in placing siblings apart (Jones & Niblett, 1985). Thus, when faced with a decision either to keep looking until a sibling placement can be found or to choose from available placements even when this means separation, the choice becomes separation. Once separation occurs (and entry in foster care is the most likely point), it is easy to maintain the separation (Ward, 1984). Little effort is spent looking for a placement that can reunify separated siblings once the problem of initial placement is solved.

Of course, these decisions are made because of difficulties with the availability of placements. The size of the posed blended family (adoptive or foster family and sibling group) is cited as a reason for not placing a sibling group together, particularly when more than 3 children enter the child welfare system at once. This problem could be remedied if there was flexibility in licensing requirements so that even if a foster family is licensed for only 2 or 3 children, the requirement can be waived when a group of siblings enters foster care. This flexibility also must be accompanied by additional resources that recruit, train and retain families who foster sibling groups.

An additional factor influencing placement decisions is sibling interaction. Sibling rivalry often precipitates the splitting of children. Perhaps one child is constantly scapegoated, or there is jealously between the children. In addition, the needs of the siblings may be different, and placing them together will meet only 1 child's needs. By separating children, families can meet the different emotional needs of children and can foster healthy interactions that reduce jealousy and scapegoating (Ward, 1984). Due to time and fiscal constraints, little intervention is usually directed to intervening in sibling dynamics while in placement. It becomes easier to separate them than to put in the effort and support necessary to keep them together.

Jones and Niblett (1985) say that to continue to make decisions about separating or maintaining sibling groups within the poverty of our current knowledge and assessment skills may pose unacceptable risks. Decisions about the placement of siblings together or apart need to be addressed in the beginning of the service continuum, instead of only at the point of adoptive placement. Professionals need to be aware of their own personal values so as to make placement decisions about siblings that are based on knowledge and research regarding siblings. Ample literature is available in the area of both adoption and sibling dynamics. In the next section, an overview of research about sibling factors and adoption outcome is provided.

ADOPTION OUTCOMES AND SIBLING PLACEMENTS

There are generally mixed results when reviewing the issue of sibling placement and adoption disruption. Some researchers suggest that placing siblings in the same home increases the risk of disruption (Boneh, 1979; Kadushin & Seidl, 1971; USRE, 1986; Boyne, Denby, Kettenring, & Wheeler, 1984). For example, Kadushin and Seidl (1971) indicate that 28% of sibling placements ended in disruption versus 1% of single child placements. However, it should be noted that a relationship between age and sibling placements was found. The average age of single placements was 4 years, and of sibling placements it was 7 years. This suggests that age at placement may have played a factor in the disruption of sibling placements.

Other researchers report no association between outcome and sibling placement (Barth et al., 1988; Rosenthal & Groze, 1990). For example, Barth et al. (1988) found that sibling placements (33%) were no more likely to disrupt than single-child placements (35%). However, sibling placements for children older than 15 tended to disrupt more than single-child placements. Related research on adoption impact by Rosenthal and Groze (1990) did not find sibling placements related to adoption impact; that is, parents did not evaluate the impact more negatively for children placed together compared to children placed alone.

Finally, some researchers (Rosenthal, Schmidt, & Conner, 1988; Festinger, 1986) found sibling placement for older children to be associated with reduced risk of disruption. For example, Festinger (1986) indicates that children who were placed alone disrupted at the rate of 10.7% compared to 5.6% for children who were placed with siblings. There were no significant differences in age of the 2 groups at the time of placement. Of the children who were placed by themselves in Festinger's study, 11.9% had siblings placed in other adoptive homes. Of the separated siblings, over 90% were believed to have moderate to severe problems. Supporting Festinger's research, Rosenthal, Schmidt, & Conner (1988) found that as the age of the child increased, the risk of disruption increased for nonsibling groups; however, for sibling groups there was no linear association between age of the child and sibling group placement. That means age is a factor for individual children but seems to have little effect when considering children who are part of a sibling group.

Research regarding adoption disruption continues to disagree about the impact of sibling placements on adoption disruption. Of the research studies reviewed, several indicated that sibling adoptions are more likely to disrupt (Kadushin & Seidl, 1971; Boneh, 1979; Boyne et al., 1984) and several indicated no increased risk for disruption (Festinger, 1986; Barth et al., 1988; Barth & Berry, 1988; Rosenthal, Schmidt, & Conner, 1988). Some studies suggest that problems in sibling placements occur only when there are other children in the home (Boneh, 1979; Barth & Berry, 1988; Rosenthal, Schmidt, & Conner, 1988). This issue can be critical in trying to unravel issues and dynamics in sibling group adoptions.

The specific research question posed in this chapter was: Are there differences in adoption outcomes between siblings placed together and siblings placed apart? Practice wisdom had suggested that initially there may be more difficulties with sibling group placements because of trying to integrate several children into the family. However, once integration takes place, it seems that over time these difficulties would decrease. In addition, it was expected that, throughout the life cycle, the siblings separated may have poorer outcomes as issues of loss, separation, and attachment to the biological families surfaced. Siblings who are together can work on the issues together while siblings who are separated cannot work on these issues with each other.

METHODOLOGY FOR EXAMINING SIBLINGS

There are unique methodological issues in measuring sibling placement (Staff, Fein, & Johnson, 1993). One issue is how to identify siblings. It is not unusual for siblings to have different last names from each other, which makes identification of them as related family members difficult. There are also issues around how to classify sibling placements. For example, if a child comes into the child welfare system, and parental rights are terminated, if the mother has another child who remains with the parent, would it be appropriate to classify the child in the system as separated from his or her sibling, although this child may not know the sibling? How would you classify children who are raised with other, nonrelated children in foster care for an extended period of time and who think that the other children are siblings? Should half-siblings be classified in the same way as full siblings? How would you classify stepsiblings? These questions and others are very difficult and are not answered here but are important considerations in reviewing the data presented.

For this study, parents were asked whether their adopted child had any known siblings, the number of known siblings, whether the adoptive placement was a sibling placement, and the number of siblings placed with the adopted child indexed for the study. Of the 71 cases in this study, the data indicate that 17% (N=12) of the children placed in adoptive homes did not have any known siblings. Of children with siblings, 46% (N=27) of the children were placed separately from their siblings, and 54%

(N=32) were placed with one or more of their siblings. Of the siblings placed together, 18 were placed with all of their siblings, and 14 were placed with some siblings. Results compare both the siblings placed separately and together as well as siblings placed apart, siblings placed with some siblings and siblings placed with all siblings. Only significant differences are highlighted in the quantitative analysis sections on child behavior and parent/child relations. These domains are highlighted because significant findings were found. Other areas such as educational functioning, contacts with the biological family, family functioning, and adoption outcomes were unremarkable (i.e., there were no statistically significant findings). Most of the results for this chapter are highlighted in the qualitative data and anecdotal information from families.

RESULTS FROM SIBLING DATA

Characteristics of the Placements

There are no gender differences in type of sibling placement. About 59% of children separated from their siblings were male compared to 38% of children placed with siblings (chi-square=1.97, p=.16). There are no racial differences. About 15% of children separated from their siblings were minority children compared to 22% of children placed with siblings. There was also no difference in abuse history and sibling placement. About 80% of children separated from their siblings were known or suspected to have been physically abused, compared to 70% of children placed with siblings. About half the children separated from their siblings were known or suspected to have been sexually abused, compared to 69% of children placed with siblings. None of these differences were statistically significant.

At the time the study began, there were no differences between the ages of children separated (mean=9.6, SD=4.3) and the ages of children placed together (mean=9.6, SD=3.3). The difference between the age at adoptive placement for children separated (mean=4.9, SD=3.6) and children placed together (mean=6.0, SD=3.1) was not significant. Children who were separated had been in the adoptive home an average of 5.3 years, and children placed together had been in the home an average of 4.5 years, a difference that is not statistically significant. There were no differences in parent characteristics (age, race, foster parent for this child) and sibling placement status.

Sibling Status and Behavior Scores

Several behaviors suggest differences over time by sibling group status, and there were some gender differences in behavior by sibling placement. Results presented in Figures 4.1 to 4.5 compare scores of the adoption sample to nonclinical norms.

Figures 4.6 to 4.10 present scores of the adoption sample compared to clinical norms (see also Chapter 3 for a discussion of the nonclinical and clinical normative groups). The closer the scores are to zero, the more similar the adoption sample scores are to the normative group.

Comparing Sibling Group Placement to Nonclinical Behavior Norms. During the first year, anxiety/depression scores for girls were least for the group of siblings placed with all their siblings and greatest for children separated from their siblings (see Figure 4.1). Over time, there was a general increase in mean scores for children placed with all the siblings. For children placed with some siblings, anxiety/depression scores decreased. Anxiety/depression scores increased slightly over time for the children separated from their siblings and remained consistently higher than scores for the children placed with their siblings. This trend was statistically significant ($F=2.28$, $p=.05$). In addition, most scores were above the score for the nonclinical group.

There was a difference in social problem scores for the different sibling group placements ($F=2.28$, $p=.05$), although there was no trend over time (see Figure 4.2). Social problem scores were highest for the children separated from their siblings and least for siblings placed together, although most scores were above the scores for the nonclinical group. Behaviors in the social problem scale included the child's acting too young for his or her age, clinging to adults or too dependent, not getting along with other kids, getting teased a lot, not being liked by other kids, and preferring to play with younger kids.

Attention problems were least for the girls for the group of siblings placed with all their siblings and greatest for the children separated from their siblings during year 1 (see Figure 4.3). Over time, the scores for the children placed with all their siblings increased and at year 4 were higher than for the group of children placed with some of their siblings. Scores for the children separated from siblings decreased slightly but remained higher over the 4-year period than for the siblings placed together. The trend was statistically significant ($F=2.29$, $p=.05$). In addition, most scores remained above the nonclinical norms during the 4-year period.

Differences in aggressive behavior over time for the girls approached statistical significance ($F=2.09$, $p=.07$; see Figure 4.4). During year 1, aggressive behavior scores were least for siblings placed with all siblings, although over time these scores increased. Aggressive behavior scores were greatest for the girls separated from their siblings and remained higher than for siblings placed together over the 4 years of the study.

For boys (see Figure 4.5), the only significant finding was in attention problems ($F=2.59$, $p=.03$). Attention problems were least for the boys for the group of siblings placed with all their siblings and greatest for the children placed with some siblings during year 1. Over time, the scores for the children placed with all their siblings increased. Scores for the children separated from siblings and placed with some siblings remained about the same over the 4-year period. In addition, most scores remained above the nonclinical norms during the 4-year period.

Comparing Sibling Group Placement to Clinical Behavior Norms. Similar to the nonclinical behavior scales, clinical behavior norms show differences between siblings placed together and apart. During the first year, anxiety/depression scores for girls were least for the group of siblings placed with all their siblings and greatest for children separated from their siblings (see Figure 4.6). Over time, there was a general increase in mean scores for children placed with all the siblings. For children placed with some siblings, anxiety/depression scores decreased. Anxiety/depression scores increased over time for the children separated from their siblings and remained consistently higher than scores for the children placed with their siblings. This trend was statistically significant ($F=2.26$, $p=.05$). In addition, most scores were below the score for the clinical group.

There was a difference in social problem scores for the different sibling group placements that approached significance ($F=3.29$, $p=.06$), although there was no trend over time (see Figure 4.7). Social problem scores were highest for the children separated from their siblings and least for siblings placed together. For the most part, scores were below scores for the clinical group for siblings placed together and above the score for the clinical group for the siblings separated.

Attention problems were least for the girls for the group of siblings placed with all their siblings and greatest for the children separated from their siblings during year 1 (see Figure 4.8). Over time, the scores for the children placed with all their siblings increased. Scores for the children separated from siblings decreased slightly but remained higher over the 4-year period than for the siblings placed together. The trend was statistically significant ($F=2.33$, $p=.04$). In addition, scores remained above the clinical norms during the 4-year period for girl children separated from their siblings and remained below the clinical norms for the girl children placed with siblings.

Differences in aggressive behavior over time for the girls approached statistical significance ($F=2.11$, $p=.07$, see Figure 4.9). During year 1, aggressive behavior scores were least for siblings placed with all siblings, although over time these scores increased. Aggressive behavior scores were greatest for the girls separated from their siblings and remained higher than for siblings placed together over the 4 years of the study. Scores for the children separated from siblings remained above the clinical norms over the 4-year period while scores for the children placed with siblings fluctuated above and below the scores for the clinical group.

For boys (see Figure 4.10), the only significant finding was in attention problems ($F=2.60$, $p=.03$). Attention problems were least for the boys for the group of siblings placed with all their siblings and greatest for the children placed with some siblings during year 1. Over time, the scores for the children placed with all their siblings increased. Scores for the children separated from siblings and placed with some siblings remained about the same over the 4-year period. In addition, most scores remained above the clinical norms during the 4-year period for siblings placed together but below the clinical norms for the children separated from siblings.

Figure 4.1
Anxiety/Depression over Time for Girls
Compared to Nonclinical Norms

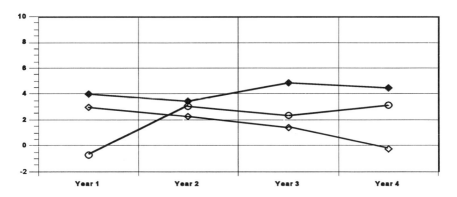

Siblings Placed Apart	Sibling Effect F=.66	p=.53
Siblings Placed With Some Sibs	Time Effect F=.48	p=.70
Siblings Placed With All Sibs	Sibling x Time Effect F=2.28	p=.05

Figure 4.2
Social Problems over Time for Girls
Compared to Nonclinical Norms

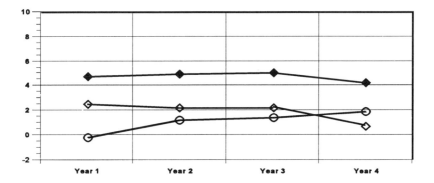

Siblings Placed Apart	Sibling Effect F=3.95	p=.03
Siblings Placed With Some Sibs	Time Effect F=.68	p=.57
Siblings Placed With All Sibs	Sibling x Time Effect F=1.65	p=.15

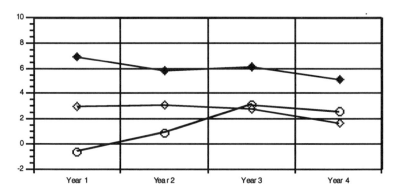

Figure 4.3
Attention Problems over Time for Girls
Compared to Nonclinical Norms

◆· Siblings Placed Apart	Sibling Effect	F=3.64	p=.04
◇ Siblings Placed With Some Sibs	Time Effect	F=.08	p=.46
⊖· Siblings Placed With All Sibs	Sibling x Time Effect	F=2.29	p=.05

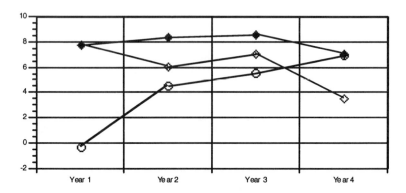

Figure 4.4
Aggressive Behavior over Time for Girls
Compared to Nonclinical Norms

◆· Siblings Placed Apart	Sibling Effect	F=.56	p=.61
◇ Siblings Placed With Some Sibs	Time Effect	F=.79	p=.51
⊖· Siblings Placed With All Sibs	Sibling x Time Effect	F=2.09	p=.07

Figure 4.5
Attention Problems over Time for Boys
Compared to Nonclinical Norms

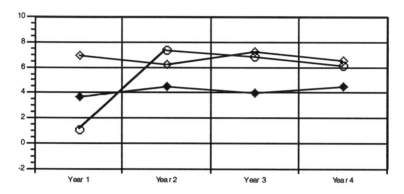

◆·	Siblings Placed Apart	Sibling Effect	F=.46	p=.63
◇	Siblings Placed With Some Sibs	Time Effect	F=2.40	p=.08
◒·	Siblings Placed With All Sibs	Sibling x Time Effect	F=2.59	p=.03

Figure 4.6
Anxiety/Depression over Time for Girls
Compared to Clinical Norms

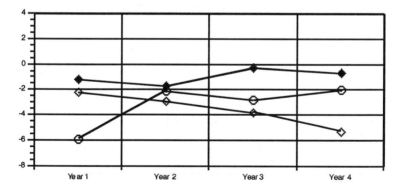

◆	Siblings Placed Apart	Sibling Effect	F=.67	p=.52
◇	Siblings Placed With Some Sibs	Time Effect	F=.46	p=.71
◒	Siblings Placed With All Sibs	Sibling x Time Effect	F=2.26	p=.05

Figure 4.7
Social Problems over Time for Girls
Compared to Clinical Norms

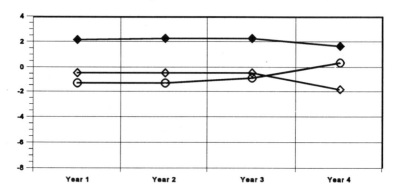

◆ Siblings Placed Apart	Sibling Effect	F=3.29	p=.06
◇ Siblings Placed With Some Sibs	Time Effect	F=.78	p=.51
⊖ Siblings Placed With All Sibs	Sibling x Time Effect	F=1.74	p=.12

Figure 4.8
Attention Problems over Time for Girls
Compared to Clinical Norms

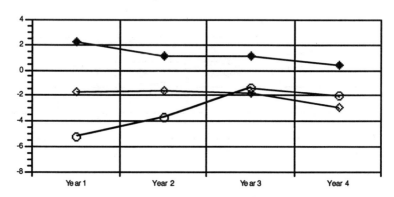

◆ Siblings Placed Apart	Sibling Effect	F=3.48	p=.05
◇ Siblings Placed With Some Sibs	Time Effect	F=.91	p=.44
⊖ Siblings Placed With All Sibs	Sibling x Time Effect	F=2.33	p=.04

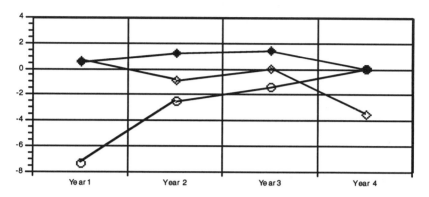

Figure 4.9
Aggressive Problems over Time for Girls
Compared to Clinical Norms

Siblings Placed Apart	Sibling Effect	F=.48 p=.62
Siblings Placed With Some Sibs	Time Effect	F=.82 p=.49
Siblings Placed With All Sibs	Sibling x Time Effect	F=2.11 p=.06

Figure 4.10
Attention Problems over Time for Boys
Compared to Clinical Norms

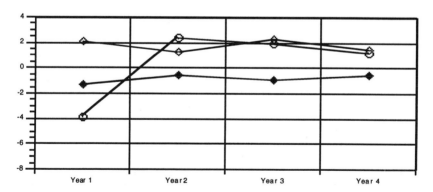

Siblings Placed Apart	Sibling Effect	F=.46 p=.64
Siblings Placed With Some Sibs	Time Effect	F=2.22 p=.09
Siblings Placed With All Sibs	Sibling x Time Effect	F=2.60 p=.03

Summary of Behavior Profiles

There are many influences on a child's behavior, including abuse history, experiences with the birth family, age at separation from the family, and so on. Results presented in this chapter suggest that sibling group status also has an effect on some behaviors. For some behaviors, it is not clear whether the behavior is a cause or consequence of sibling group status. For example, it is not clear whether female children are more likely to be placed separately from their siblings if they show attention problems, aggressive behavior, or social problems. It is clear, however, that these problems remain higher for the siblings separated than for the siblings placed together. Anxiety/depression for the girls may be a concrete manifestation of the existential crisis promoted by being separated from one's sibling(s). Attention problem patterns over time were different for the boys and girls. Consistent for both boys and girls was that the children placed with all their siblings increased their attention problem scores over time. However, whereas the females separated from their siblings had the highest score over time, the boys separated from their siblings had the lowest scores over time.

The Effect of Sibling Placements on Parent/Child Relations

There were significant differences between sibling placement status and several variables assessing parent/child relations. Results are presented in Table 4.1. For the item asking about how the parent got along with the child, initially, scores were the same for children placed apart from their siblings and children placed together. Over time, relations slightly improve for children who are placed apart and get worse for siblings placed together.

For evaluation of parent/child communication, initially, scores were the same for children placed apart from their siblings and children placed together. Over time, relations remain about the same for children who are placed apart and get worse for siblings placed together.

Finally, for the item that asks whether the parent feels respected by the child, there are significant differences between sibling placement status. Parents report higher scores for siblings placed apart and lower scores for siblings placed together. This difference between the groups remains over the 4-year period. While other items do not reach statistical significance, results suggest that both trust and how close the parent feels to the child have the same pattern as getting along with the child, communication with the child, and trust of the child. Anxious attachment is greater in children placed apart and decreases slightly over the 4 years, whereas for siblings placed together it is lower and increases slightly over the 4 years. Even with the increase, anxious attachment remains greater for siblings who are separated. Avoidant attachment is greater for siblings placed together and decreases slightly during the fourth year whereas for siblings who are separated it is slightly higher over time.

Table 4.1
Repeated MANOVA for Siblings Placed Together and Siblings
Placed Apart on Parent-Child Relationship Items

	Mean Score				
	Siblings Apart	**Siblings Together**	**Effect**	**F**	**P**
Getting along					
Year 1	3.6	3.6	Sibling Status	6.32	.00
Year 2	3.8	3.4	Time	3.78	.01
Year 3	3.7	3.2	Sib*Time	4.06	.00
Year 4	3.7	3.1			
Communication					
Year 1	3.3	3.3	Sibling Status	1.63	.21
Year 2	3.4	3.0	Time	6.70	.00
Year 3	3.2	2.9	Sib*Time	2.89	.04
Year 4	3.2	2.7			
Trust					
Year 1	3.1	3.0	Sibling Status	1.35	.25
Year 2	3.0	2.9	Time	4.66	.00
Year 3	3.0	2.7	Sib*Time	.76	.52
Year 4	2.9	2.5			
Respect					
Year 1	3.4	3.2	Sibling Status	3.71	.06
Year 2	3.4	3.2	Time	5.40	.00
Year 3	3.3	2.9	Sib*Time	1.60	.19
Year 4	3.2	2.6			
Closeness					
Year 1	3.6	3.6	Sibling Status	1.02	.32
Year 2	3.5	3.2	Time	7.09	.00
Year 3	3.4	3.1	Sib*Time	.79	.50
Year 4	3.2	3.1			
Anxious Attachment					
Year 1	4.4	2.8	Sibling Status	1.97	.17
Year 2	4.5	3.2	Time	.83	.48
Year 3	4.4	3.8	Sib*Time	1.21	.31
Year 4	4.1	3.3			
Avoidant Attachment	2.6	2.7	Sibling Status	.05	.82
Year 1	2.5	2.7	Time	.37	.77
Year 2	2.9	2.7	Sib*Time	.59	.62
Year 3	2.8	2.3			
Year 4					

The differences in parent/child relations provide partial evidence of the importance of the sibling bond. The sibling group develops a strong subsystem that affects the quality of parent/child relations. Children separated from their siblings are easier to influence because the parent is trying to build a relationship with only 1 child. Trying to build a relationship with more than 1 child is difficult. Thus, sibling status influences some aspects of parent/child relations.

THE QUALITATIVE AND ANECDOTAL INFORMATION FROM FAMILIES

The qualitative data for families that adopted siblings placed together compared to families who adopted a child separated from his or her sibling(s) reflect some common, broad themes such as the family's love for, and commitment to, the child, issues of the child's sense of security and ability to trust others, the importance of having complete background information on the adopted child, and the role of external support services in facilitating the adjustment and ongoing growth of both the child as an individual and the family as a whole. The primary difference between the families in which the children were placed with siblings and those families where the children were placed separately is the sense that the families who adopted 1 or more siblings have a more tempered view, or more realistic expectations, about the adjustment process and the degree to which the children will experience emotional and behavioral difficulties. Children who do not have any biological siblings seem to experience the least amount of emotional or behavioral disruption. Following is a summary of the responses from the parents to several open-ended questions analyzed by sibling status.

Children Placed Separately from Biological Siblings

The 1990 data reveal that of the 27 families in which the child was placed separately from his or her siblings, 33% (N=9) reported having to deal with serious behavioral problems. Serious behavioral problems are considered to include out-of-control, destructive, or violent types of behaviors. By 1993, improvement was noted in 4 of the 9 cases. Examples of this shift to a more positive pattern of behaviors are reflected in the following statements.

In 1990 the parent of a child who was adopted at age 8 and had been in the adoptive placement 6 years and separated from 5 siblings stated (in response to asking what was different from the parent's expectations):

The intensity with which she clings to negative behaviors. The impact the behaviors have had on my relationships with friends.

Other concerns were stated as:

the manner in which she sets herself up to fail. She does not take direction and seems only to learn from the most traumatic personal experiences... the way she seems to set up adversarial relations between significant people in her life. "Hating" one so that she can get closer to the other. Then reversing that when it helps the particular situation.

In 1991 this parent was concerned

that her academic skills and social skills may not be such that she will be employable one day. That her disorganization and poor memory may not allow her to adequately meet her health needs. That she wants so much to be liked that she is very vulnerable even now.

In 1992, when the family moved to a new area, the mother comments:

Simona has made many friends here. This was difficult for her in [another town]. This has allowed her to grow beyond our relationship. She has less nightmares, flashbacks and fears of her Dad.

By 1993, the child's positive qualities include:

conversational skills with many age groups. Good short term relationships.

Another parent adopted a child who was 10 at placement. The child had been in the home 2 years and was separated from 1 other sibling in 1990. The parent reported:

We expected to go through an initial adjustment period where there would be some testing and acting out behaviors and then have a fairly smooth life. The first 18 months followed this pattern. Then everything fell apart due to his extreme fears and flashbacks from his past. . . . The unpredictability of his mood swings-having him go out of control, destroying property, threatening my life over seemingly small issues. Even though I realize this came from an inability to cope with his fears and past, I still have trouble trusting him. I feel the need to stay on top of things and be prepared to deal with a violent episode.

By 1991 the parents had not expected to go "over the same issues again and again--trust is especially hard for our son." The parent also notes: "He works hard to succeed--*always* comes home from school and gets on with his homework. Really cares that he does well in school."

In 1992 the parent wrote:

Two years ago was a very rough period for our son and family. Through weekly therapy sessions he gained a lot of ground. The past year and a half have gone fairly well. He only loses control about once a year (and) . . . fear of failing . . . seems to be the underlying cause. We should have started therapy sooner--before his behavior had gotten out of control. Understanding that fear triggers angry behavior would have helped.

Finally, during the last year the mother indicated "impulsiveness" as the only concern.

Generally, the positive changes noted in these cases is attributed, in part, to support from sources outside the family. As a result of such interventions, it seems that the families were able to come to a better understanding of the issues underlying the child's behavior and to respond accordingly.

The data reveal 2 cases where problems persisted and, in fact, deteriorated to the point where, in 1 case, the child was removed from the home by court order. In the second case, the child's behavior and history of abuse triggered memories of his adoptive mother's own abusive past. Consequently, tension and conflict between the adoptive mother and son seemed ongoing. In addition, the father noted that his wife "was forced into a depression and [that] she has been seeing a psychologist for almost three years." The father also states, "They shake their heads and say that he was a very poor placement in our home." Interestingly, despite the relatively dismal prognoses for these children and their family relationships, neither adoption was terminated.

For children separated from their biological siblings, more moderate types of behavior problems were described by 30% (N=8) of the families in 1990 and by 37% (N=10) in 1993. These behaviors include a tendency to be pushy or bossy, lying, immaturity, anger, and impulsiveness. The slight increase in numbers over the 4 years reflects two complementary shifts in the data: (1) decrease in the number of serious behavioral problems and (2) an increase of behavioral concerns not noted in the first year of the study.

Over the 4-year period of the study, 7 of the families describing some moderate behavior problems also identify as a concern a lack of trust, a sense of insecurity, or a need to control others or be the center of attention. These behaviors are viewed often as an issue related to the behavior needing to be addressed. Following are some examples taken from the data:

Her insecurity in our love at times. Also she tries so hard to control the household, myself, and the other children. She thinks she's the mother figure and tries to "boss" everyone. (1990, child placed at age 6, in the home 4 years, and separated from 2 other siblings)

She wants friends, but due to being in a small school her actions from kindergarten have followed her. She is known for being pushy in line and always wanting to be first. (1991, same child as preceeding)

The fact that it has taken so long for the child to bond, still at times pushes away. (1991, child placed as an infant with developmental delays, in placement 5 years, and separated from 9 other siblings)

From the reports I expected a rotten child, but she is your basic kid that needs a lot of love. I have a hard time getting her to listen and not wanting to be the boss. (1991, child placed at age 11, in placement 3 years, and separated from 3 other siblings)

Bad behaviors (extreme) keep popping up. . . . He's such a neat adorable child, very loving. He seems more secure since the adoption. (1991, child placed at age 1, in the home 5 years, and separated from 3 other siblings)

We were hoping he would feel more secure than he does. He's afraid of losing us. With being foster parents the foster children remind him of things before his adoption, like leaving us weekends. He's very concerned about family members. When there is an illness he is very concerned about that person. (1992, same child as preceding)

Of note in this group is that some parents did not experience difficulties with the adopted child's behavior; rather, their biological child became "jealous." In 1990 in one family, the parent noted that she had not expected the jealousy to continue for "so long." Interestingly, in 1992, the data seem to suggest that a second adoption occurred since 1990, and, coincidentally, her biological son was "having problems." Although the data do not elaborate on the issues with the biological son, it would seem reasonable for issues to arise, as another person in the home would require that time and attention be redirected to helping meet the needs of this new person. As this was a special needs adoption, likely an even greater amount of attention was shifted from the biological child to the adopted child. While the data are not explicit as to the reason for resentment, another adoptive parent states: "This adoption has been very hard on our biological children. Even now after 5 years they resent him. It's also been hard on our marriage and on me personally." Adapting to accommodate a new person into the family is stressful; energy expended to meet the needs of an adopted child may result in less energy and attention to other children in the home who preceded the adoptive placement.

Despite the large number of families working hard to deal with the emotional, behavioral, and developmental needs of their adopted children, 37% (N=10) of the cases in 1990 reported only positive feelings surrounding the adoption. For example:

She has brought great joy to the lives of all who know her. This is not just a platitude, but a fact! (child adopted at age 10, in adoptive placement 9 years, and separated from 2 other siblings)

Just having him around. His personality. Keeping us active. (child adopted at age 2 with developmental delays, in the home 3 years and separated from one other sibling)

The child's adaptability was very smooth. She was eager to have her "new" family. (child adopted at age 7, in adoptive placement for 2 years, and separated from 1 sibling)

We have become a really close family. My husband and I have had to work very hard and closely together to help our son. It's been great. (child placed at age 2 with developmental delays, in the home for 9 years, and separated from 1 sibling)

He's been "ours" almost since his first day of foster placement. We're the only parents he really has ever known. (biracial child placed as an infant, in adoptive placement 3 years, and separated from 6 siblings)

[He] completed our family and [the adoption] made the child feel that this was truly his home. (child placed at age 5, in the home 4 years, and separated from 1 sibling)

Of the 10 families reporting only positive comments in 1990, 6 remained consistent in their positive perspectives regarding their child's personality and behavior throughout the 4 years of the study. Of these 6 cases, 4 were families who had adopted children who had some physical or mental disability. In these cases it would seem reasonable to think that the disability would be of primary importance, therefore removing the focus from any behavioral issues. An alternative explanation may be that physical limitations associated with the disability may inhibit certain acting-out types of behaviors that might be observed in other children.

Children Placed with 1 or More Siblings

Children placed with 1 or more siblings make up 32 of the adoptive families in this study. While children in this group exhibit some of the same problems in terms of disruptive behaviors, difficulty in trusting, a sense of fear of loss, and developmental disabilities, the data seem to generally reflect a slightly more balanced view of the impact of the children's problems than in those families in which children are placed separately from their biological siblings. The difference seems to rest in the area of expectations. In other words, although the degree of upset or disruption associated with the placement of children in some cases in this group is greater than for some of those where the children are placed separately from their biological siblings, the outcome was consistent with the expectations that the families had regarding the adoption experience, as evidenced in these comments:

Nothing we didn't expect. . . . Questions were answered honestly and to our satisfaction. This child has been a joy. He is a loving, caring, compassionate, energetic, ornery nine year old. We wouldn't change a thing. . . . Julian is a very special young man/boy. He can do extremely well in school academically, he needs a lot of structure behaviorally. (child placed at age 5, in adoptive placement 4 years, and the parent did not specify the number of siblings placed together)

[What has been] most helpful [is the] background information I received on Catalina. It helped very much as [I] tried to understand her many fears. (child placed at age 3 with 1 of 3 siblings and in the adoptive home 5 years)

For Katrina there has been no difference from my expectations. . . . [There had been] differences from her brother in toilet training [she was very hard to train], and she is a very active child who climbs and gets into things more than all 3 brothers combined. (child placed as an infant with 1 of 4 siblings, and in the home 4 years)

[The] adoption worker gave information and resources on adopting older children which was very helpful. . . . The differences I have experienced have more to do with what other parents [of biological children] also experience. I don't think it has much to do with Marius being adopted per se. He is ADD with hyperactivity-it makes school and around home stressed sometimes . . . . He is now on medication. He is also a bed wetter--this gets "old" after a while. (biracial child placed at age 5 with 1 of 5 siblings, and in adoptive placement 7 years)

They [the workers] were both very supportive. Spending a great deal of time helping us adjust. I did not expect to feel the deep love for this child . . . . So far this has been an easy adjustment. (child placed at age 10 with 2 of 2 siblings, and in the home 1 year)

A negative experience is reflected in the discordance between expectations and reality:

Our worker was pretty insistent that we take 2 siblings--older brother has been a problem and has not bonded with our family. We would have been much better off with just our daughter in placement. (child placed at age 10 with 1 of 1 siblings and in the home 3 years)

I didn't have actual services but I did check with her when the mother was trying to contact the children . . . . My kids have been harder to handle than I thought. (child placed at age 4 with 2 of 2 siblings and in the adoptive placement 9 years)

We were not told about Carolina's behavior problems and didn't prepare ourselves to deal with them. (child placed at age 4 with 1 of 1 sibling and in the home 2 years)

It seems that the expectations held by parents are related, at least in part, to the preparation that they received from workers before the adoption. As one family states:

I really think adoptive parents should be required to have more training on adopting older special needs children that would include hearing other parents that have done it say "it's not like the Brady Bunch." I was under the mistaken idea that you could adopt a child, give it lots of love and it would make everything all right for them. That is not always true. Some things you can never make right for them. It's not a guarantee that if you love them that they will love and trust you and bond with you because sometimes that doesn't happen. (minority child placed at age 10 with 1 of 1 sibling and in the home 4 years)

A recurring theme that appears to emerge in the data is that of the siblings adopted, often one child's behavior is more problematic than that of the others, even if all children are experiencing difficulty adjusting to a new family situation.

Things have gone pretty well with Marianna. She is a pretty, sensitive girl who wants to please everyone. We know she loves us. Academically she improves year by year although it's hard for her. Now her brother Elija was a very different story. (minority child placed at age 10 with 1 of 1 siblings and in the home 4 years)

She's loving, caring, sharing, beautiful, stubborn, mouthy, helpful, she's been like my right arm since my illness last June. She's growing up with just a touch of little girl left. Our son is stubborn as a mule, hard to teach, rebellious, yet wanting to grow up, loving, sharing, loves to go to church. (child placed at age 3 with 1 of 1 sibling and in adoptive placement 9 years)

To be truthful, we wanted to adopt our daughter very badly, but were told that her brother must stay with her . . . . [Her] brother has been a problem and has not bonded with our family. (child adopted at age 10 with 1 of 1 sibling and in the home 3 years)

[Her] twin sister was also adopted by us . . . . Rosie appears to have little reaction [to seeing siblings]. Her twin, on the other hand, reflects very negative behaviors afterwards. (child adopted at age 7 with 1 of 4 siblings and in the adoptive home 9 years)

My kids are hard to handle and resentful. (child adopted at age 4 with 2 of 2 siblings and in the adoptive placement 9 years)

In two cases the behaviors of the more disruptive child were so severe that the child was removed from the adoptive home and placed in foster care. While this action did not eliminate problems for the other children in the adoptive home, in both cases the situation was much improved as one parent commented:

Since he [the older brother] has left the home, Jule's Jekyll/Hyde personality has almost disappeared. (child adopted at age 7 with 3 of 3 siblings and in the home 5 years)

In one other case the adoptive parents talked about preparing for the adoption of a sibling group by becoming aware of the adjustment issues with which the children may be confronted. Unexpectedly, the parents found that they were the ones who were having the difficulty adjusting:

We expected the kids would have many adjustment problems based on what we were told by social worker. That was a laugh. They had each other [3 sisters, Monica is the middle child] and Gene and I had the adjustment problems! Each problem that came up was an absolute major crisis and it took us three or four years to realize that you just go from day to day. Developing perspective was the hardest part. (child adopted at age 6 with 2 of 4 siblings and in the adoptive home 10 years)

Two families commented explicitly on the impact that the negative behaviors of the adopted child may have or are having on the parents' biological children. One parent had not expected to see the positive impact on her children. This parent states, "He has brought out qualities in our older children that are very good and that I'm not sure we would ever have seen had we not adopted troubled children." In the second case, the parent expressed concern regarding "the emotional damage I fear may be happening to my biological children."

Forty percent (N=12) of the cases in the first year of the study reported purely positive feelings about the adopted child. Parents seemed to express a real sense of joy or infatuation with their adopted children. Some comments include:

She is wonderful. April has brought so much love and joy into our lives. (child adopted as infant with 1 of 2 siblings and in the home for 6 years)

I had no idea that we could grow to love and depend on each other as much as we do . . .

watching and feeling the bond grow between us. (child adopted at age 3 with 1 of 3 siblings and in adoptive placement 5 years)

Shannah and her adoptive mom (me) are so much alike it's scary! Our temperament, appearance, attitudes. She says it's special to trust and like a mom now! yes! yes! (child adopted at age 8 with 5 of 5 siblings and in the adoptive home 2 years)

Becoming parents and having the chance to share our love with two wonderful children (child adopted at age 5 with 1 of 1 sibling and in the home 3 years)

Over time, there is some shift in the positive reporting, which may be reflective of moving beyond the "honeymoon" stage of the relationship. Shifts were noted in the other direction as well, where parents were able to articulate an increasingly positive perception of the child or children. By year 4, 28% (N=9) of the families were providing information on the child that focused more on the positive aspects of the child's personality or behavior.

Children Who Do Not Have Any Known Biological Siblings

Of the 12 placed who do not have biological siblings, serious behavioral problems were noted in only one case during the first year of the data collection. In this case, the child's behavior echoes that of many children in the other two groupings. Specifically, this child is described as having a:

need for control of others, manipulative . . . periodic tantrums/severe emotional displays . . . [a] willingness to inflict hurt and destruction upon people who don't give her what she wants. She can be very cruel and destructive. (child adopted at age 4 and in the adoptive home 11 years)

It should be noted that the adoptive parents are also clear about their love for their child and their ability to see her positive qualities. For example, the parents of the preceding child state:

She's a wonderful person who has come into our lives for us to know and watch grow. It's the beauty of life before our very eyes. It's the thrill of seeing her develop into what she is, the unique person with her unique observation of the world. [She is] very intelligent, active, adventuresome, fearless, loves animals and is very good with them.

Two other cases citing some degree of behavioral difficulties emerge in 1991. One case indicates moderate problems involving a lack of desire "to follow house rules" as well as some problems at school. Although not explicitly stated, the 1993 data suggest that these issues remain constant as the adoptive parent reiterates concerns regarding the child's "attitude in life" and "not having an education."

The third case reveals an interesting profile of the adoption relationship. In the first year of the study, the comments do not reflect any negative characteristics of the child, but a concern about "being a good parent" is expressed. Moving beyond the initial phase of adjustment, the behaviors associated with the child's diagnosis of attention deficit with hyperactivity disorder (ADHD) begin to emerge, and concern is expressed about the child's problems related to school, peer relationships (aggression, primarily), and difficulties at home.

Including the two additional cases identified following the first year of the study, moderate to serious behavioral problems occurred in 3 additional families in this group. Perhaps more significantly in this group is the number of children who were identified as having disabilities including serious medical problems, developmental delays, and hyperactivity. Families identifying stress related to such issues constitute 67% (N=8) of this group. Concern about planning for the child's future is an emergent theme in this group. In one case the family did not know whether they should be planning for "his future or his funeral." Furthermore, the parent states: "What kind of future will he have? It is hard to know how to plan for his future when his medical condition has no known prognosis. We don't know if he will live to be an adult, or how severely he may be handicapped by them." Although most of the medical conditions are not as severe as this one, the adoptive parents expressed worry about planning for the future medical and mental needs of their child. The primary burden or source of stress and frustration for families with children who have disabilities seems to be outside the family and with other "systems." Specific issues pertain to the access and cost of health and social services. Such themes are reflected in the following comments:

Our child has had a lot of medical problems. . . . All of this required a lot of adjustments for all of us. . . . Getting medical care . . . is difficult, because many doctors/hospitals/clinics do not want the hassle of . . . waiting many months for payment. We still (after living here 3 years) have not found an ophthalmologist or optometrist for him. (child adopted as infant who has been in the adoptive placement 10 years)

The grant [subsidy] per month was almost found by accident. [There have been] so many changes in rules and forms and requirements in the 15 years we've had Diana. We feel if we've accidentally filled out a form incorrectly--we'll be hauled to prison. . . . We've been on a roller coaster each year not knowing the rules for medical and financial subsidies--new income levels, forms, workers etc. (child adopted as infant and in the home 15 years)

We are with her 24 hours a day except for school as nobody knows how to deal with [her] handicap. [We] could never find [a] physical therapist or occupational therapist for her. Even the YWCA wouldn't let her come and swim. (child adopted as infant and in the placement 12 years)

In the last case, the comment highlights that for families with adopted children who have disabilities, the source of frustration and stress for the family is often viewed as external to the family. In other words, whereas families with other types of special needs children report issues regarding the child and his or her behavior, families of the disabled child comment more frequently on concerns for the child's future and the frustration at the lack of support or services for their child.

All parents in this group were able to identify positive characteristics they appreciated in their children, despite health and behavioral problems. Nine of the families reported on their child's positive qualities only; this percentage remains constant over the 4 years of the study.

Unique to this group are statements by the adoptive parents that suggest that "adoption" is a nonissue. For example:

Adoption is *Not* important--she *is* our child! (child adopted as infant and in the placement 12 years)

We tend to forget that Diana is adopted. We feel no differently toward the other biological daughter or Diana. (child adopted as infant and in the home 13 years)

In fact, some families have gone as far as to almost deny the nonbiological tie to the family:

The fact of Eduardo's adoption is simply not a factor in our family. He is a part of our family just as the biological children are. (child adopted as an infant and in the adoptive home 9 years)

Jude is and always has been our own flesh and blood. It was just a matter of a name change at adoption. She gave and gives me the tender loving care that all "true" mothers have in carrying a newborn. She has satisfied a nurturing nature in myself since I've never given birth. (child adopted at age 1 and in the placement 14 years)

This latter parent states in 1990 that adopting Jude "has fulfilled a need to nurture a little baby." Of note is that as potential conflicts and behavioral problems began to emerge in this individual's teen years, the family chose to move to a smaller town. The move was regarded as a positive change for the family as Jude's behaviors dissipated, and her school performance improved.

SUMMARY

The data provided limited support for the expectation that siblings placed together would have better outcomes than siblings separated. There were some differences between siblings placed apart and siblings placed together on several dimensions of parent/child relations. There also were significant behavior differences. However, overall, there does not appear to be strong differences between the siblings placed together and the siblings separated on most variables studied with this sample. Does this suggest that current policy or practice should be modified? Definitely not. It may suggest that once a decision has been made to separate siblings, outcomes for the children for whom this decision is made can be positive. It also may mean that by the time a decision has been made for the children to be adopted, the differences that were expected were negligible because the children had spent some time in foster care in other family systems that affected the sibling relationship. While results suggest limited differences, it is important to continue to emphasize in policy and practice the continuance of sibling ties. Some issues that siblings have about being separated will not show up on standardized measures, such as the existential longing that children have for the misplaced sibling. Both theory and research suggest a more careful examination of this issue of sibling placement in policy and practice. These issues are explored in more detail in Chapter 7.

5

Physically and Sexually Abused Adoptees

INTRODUCTION

Most special needs adoptive children entered adoption through the child welfare system, and many have experienced neglect and/or abuse as part of their preadoptive history. In the recent past, children became involved in the child welfare system due to parental neglect, although over the last decade increasing numbers of children enter care from physical and sexual abuse. About half (44%) of child maltreatment reports are substantiated as neglect, with 24% substantiated physical abuse and 15% substantiated as sexual abuse (National Center on Child Abuse and Neglect, [NCCAN], 1993). The number of reports of child maltreatment more than doubled from the 1970s to the 1980s (American Humane Association, 1988), with sexual abuse reports rising at a faster rate than other types of maltreatment (Lie & McMurtry, 1991).

These increases in reports have also resulted in an increase in children in substitute care. According to Tatara (1993), the substitute care population increased by 7.1% in fiscal year (FY) 1987, 9.0% in FY 1988, 10.4% in FY 1989 and 11.8% in FY 1990. This increase translates into about 300,000 children in substitute care in 1987 increasing to 406,000 in care by 1990. At the same time it is important to note that with federal policy mandates (e.g., P.L. 96-272) and the development of an array of family preservation and support services, most maltreated children remain with their families or are reunited with the family system. Only when efforts at family preservation and family reunification are not successful, will the permanency plan become adoption. Estimates are that less than 10% (Finch, Fanshel, & Grundy, 1986; McMurty & Lie, 1992; Tatara, 1993) of children in the child welfare system will move to adoption as the permanency plan. While there are no accurate data, the Voluntary Cooperative Information System (VCIS) estimates that over 20,000 children are placed from foster care into adoption for the most recent year available (Tatara, 1993).

Thus, many of the children who become available for adoption have a legacy of neglect or abuse. It is very difficult to assess the effects of child abuse and neglect; often there are multiple conditions associated or correlated with child maltreatment, such as poverty and community deficits (Belsky, 1980; Costin, Bell, & Downs, 1991). In addition, the methodological and sampling difficulties make it precarious to draw conclusions. However, it is possible to identify effects for some children (DePanfilis & Salus, 1992).

Some behaviors that have been documented about deprived or neglected children include listlessness, aggressiveness, antisocial behavior, difficulties with attachment, and academic difficulties (Yarrow, 1961, cited in Sack & Dale, 1982; Rutter 1972; Erickson, Egeland, & Pianta, 1989; Wodarski et al., 1990). Abused children can demonstrate a range of socioemotional problems, such as acute anxiety, depression, panic on separation, provocation, testing, punishment-seeking, poor impulse control, marginal peer relationships, aggressiveness, attachment difficulties, and abuse fantasies about the caretakers (Yates, 1981; Green, 1978; George & Main, 1979; Kinard, 1980; Erickson, Egeland, & Pianta, 1989; Wodarski et al., 1990; Harper, 1991; Kaverola et al., 1993). Significant impairment in school achievement and cognitive functioning has been reported (Brahal, Waterman, & Martin, 1981; Christiansen, 1980; Hoffman-Plotkin & Twentyman, 1984; Kline, 1977; Vondra, Barnett, & Cicchetti, 1990; Wodarski et al., 1990) for maltreated children. Maltreated children also tend to have difficulties with self-esteem and self-concept (Kaufman & Cicchetti, 1989; Oates, Forrest, & Peacock, 1985; Kinard, 1980), although contradictory findings have also been reported (Elmer, 1977). Effects of abuse can last long beyond childhood (Beitchman et al., 1992; Busby et al., 1993; Moeller, Bachmann, & Moeller, 1993), and some difficulties become more problematic with age for children who have been physically abused (Wodarski et al., 1990).

While considerable research has addressed causes and consequences of child maltreatment, little is known about adoption outcomes for maltreated children. Given that a significant portion of special needs adoptees experience abuse or neglect as part of their preadoptive history, it is important to explore the effects of this history on adoption outcomes.

ADOPTION OUTCOMES FOR MALTREATED CHILDREN

Adoption outcomes include the disruption of the adoption after placement as well as the postplacement functioning of the child (or children) and the adopted family. Several studies suggest that a history of sex abuse may place a child at increased risk for disruption (Schmidt, 1985; Smith & Howard, 1991). In general, postplacement functioning of maltreated children has been positive. Kadushin (1967) conducted one of the earliest follow-up studies of children adopted with a history of abuse and neglect. Children were adopted at 7.2 years, on average, and were 13.9 years old at the time of the study. They had been removed from their homes at an average age of 3.5 years because of abuse or neglect. He found that parent satisfaction with the adoption was high and that the adoption experiences were similar to those of other families who adopted children with no known maltreatment history. He discusses how an adoptive family can promote healing and at least a partial reversal of trauma to children.

Reid et al. (1987) examined adoption outcomes for maltreated children, over half of whom were abused and 8% of whom were neglected. Many of the children had significant behavior problems. At the time of the study, about one-fourth of the children were out of the home, either in residential treatment or living out of the home, but the adoption was not legally terminated. Seventy-five percent of the placements remained intact, although parents were stressed in dealing with behavior difficulties. The authors did not differentiate the effects of abuse compared to the effects of neglect. While problems were identified, most adoptions would still be classified as successful.

Berry and Barth (1989), in their analysis of over 900 cases of older child adoption, indicated that over 60% of children were physically abused, 80% were neglected, and 33% were sexually abused. The majority of children evidenced significant behavior problems. However, even with the traumatic backgrounds and behavior difficulties, most families (86%) were satisfied and said they would adopt again.

Rosenthal and Groze (1992) conducted a follow-up of about 800 special needs adoptive families in a multistate area. About one-third of the children had a known or suspected history of sexual abuse, and most had a preadoptive history of physical abuse. While overall results were very positive, sexual abuse was significantly associated with more negative adoption outcomes, particularly the impact of the adoption on the family.

In the best empirical study that specifically focused on the effects of abuse on adoption outcome, Smith and Howard (1994) compared adoption outcomes for children who were sexually abused (N=35) to children with no sex abuse history (N=113). Sexual abuse was associated with more foster care placements, greater frequency and type of behavior problems, and more attachment difficulties.

CHILD MALTREATMENT AND THE ADOPTIVE FAMILY

Child maltreatment prior to the adoptive placement can have a significant effect on the child, which, in turn, affects his or her functioning in the family. The areas in which abuse becomes most apparent is in children's behavior, cognition, and affect. Problems in these areas can become an additional source of stress to the adoptive families. These three areas are reviewed here; some of this material is also presented in Chapter 1.

Child Behavior

Child maltreatment affects the individual coping style of the child. Children develop survival behaviors to both deal with abuse as well as deal with various placements in the child welfare system (Donley, 1990). Many of these survival behaviors are problematic as adoptive families try to manage the behavior. Sexually abused children may not have good boundaries about their bodies, both with people inside the family and with people outside the family. They often experience inappropriate sexual behavior and confusion about sexual norms (Finkelhor & Browne, 1985; Smith & Howard, 1994). Physically abused and neglected children may not respect personal space, including property. It is not unusual for them to destroy their own belongings or the possessions of others. They may hoard items or not place much value on property, impulsively taking things that are not their own for no particular reason or "stealing" within the family. It is not unusual for maltreated children to be aggressive and to have a difficult time sitting still, paying attention for any length of time, or following through with task and activities until completion. When frustrated or under stress, these children cope by relying on their survival behaviors. These behaviors often last many years after adoptive placement and can be quite discouraging to the parents and other members of the family system who expect them to change over time.

Child Affect

Abused children often experience deficits in their interpersonal and social skills. They may not be able to express a wide range of feelings. Some children become familiar with only one feeling, such as anger or depression, and are unable or unwilling to experience a wider range of emotions. Often, children have difficulty developing the language for expressing what they feel, and affective responses are translated into behavior. The emotional language of children is their behavior. Parents may experience the children as passive and apathetic or as hostile and angry. Their response to situations may seem out of proportion to the event. Often there is little reciprocity in affection. There may be incongruence between facial expression and feelings; for example, the child may frown but say he or she is happy. This incongruence is a survival mechanism where children learn to mask their feelings. Parents can become disconcerted when trying to sort out feelings, expression of feelings, and the behavior of their adopted child who was abused.

Child Cognition

Based on early life experiences with caregivers, children develop a cognitive model of themselves, their caregivers, and the world around them (Bowlby, 1969, 1973, 1988; Main, Kaplan, & Cassidy, 1985; Main & Weston, 1981). This model is then transferred to other relationships. When these early experiences result in abuse or neglect, cognitive models can become negative and filled with anxiety, anger, confusion, or depression. The children have experienced the world as an unsafe and unpredictable place. They may believe that they can trust others only to hurt or ignore them. They internalize negative models, which subsequently affect their self-esteem and interpersonal relations. Negative working models of relationships with adults may lead them to distance themselves from adult relationships. Often, parents experience this distancing as a lack of reciprocity in the parent/child relations. The children may have a tendency to withdraw from relations. In other instances, their working models of relations is that they can expect abuse. Thus, they invite abuse and can be very skillful in getting parents, siblings, or other caregivers to perpetuate abuse in their lives. On the other hand, they may be overly clinging and demanding in relations or overly aggressive and hurtful. It should be kept in mind that children are acting on the cognitive models they have of interpersonal relations. These negative models of other relationships can result in poor or inadequate relations with adults, peers, or siblings.

Effects of Maltreatment on the Adoptive Family

It is not the maltreatment history per se that families have a difficult time with, although some families struggle when the child is known to have a history of sexual abuse. More often the effect of the history can be troublesome. The effects of the maltreatment can be an additional stressor to the family. Parents often do not experience positive and consistent acceptance by their children. The children often do not adhere to defined and enforced limits of their behavior. In addition, children rarely experience only one type of abuse. Often, they are victims of multiple abuse, and the effects of physical abuse, sexual abuse, and neglect overlap. It is also important to keep in mind that the age of the abuse, its type, and its severity interact. Some abuse is more traumatic depending on the age of the child. In addition, effects of abuse differ by severity. So, families may struggle with managing the emotional and behavioral complications of abuse and neglect over a long period of time.

Families can successfully parent these children if they have knowledge of the abuse beforehand, and they get the training they need to understand the effects of abuse on their adopted child. However, information is a resource to the family only when the history of abuse or neglect is made known before the child is placed; difficulties are encountered when the information was not shared or not known before the placement. Barth (1988) suggests that adoptive placements are put at greater risk for disruption when families were not informed in advance about a child's sexual abuse. But, knowing this information is often more complicated than it appears. It is not that the information is deliberately withheld from adoptive parents. Often, as in the case of sexual abuse, a history of abuse is suspected after a child has behaved in a provocative manner. Unfortunately, the provocative behavior in sexual abuse is often sexual. This is the one behavior that seems to place adoption stability at greatest risk, particularly if the behavior is defined as sex-offending behavior (Groze, Young, & Corcran-Rumppe, 1991). Children with a preadoptive history of sexual abuse seem to be particularly traumatized and may have the greatest difficulty with postplacement adjustment (McNamara & McNamara, 1990).

METHODOLOGY FOR EXAMINING MALTREATMENT

Two questions on the survey probed preadoptive history of abuse. Parents were asked, Was your child physically abused prior to adoptive placement? and Was your child sexually abused prior to adoptive placement? Parents could respond Yes, No, or Suspected.

There are some problems with the collection of abuse data. First, the study relied on parent reports, which may differ from official records on the children. Second, no attempt was made to ascertain the severity or degree of abuse. Third, the age at which the abuse occurred was not reported. Fourth, no data were collected about the child's history of neglect. Thus, the data that are reported represent only very crude measures of abuse history. However, the strength of the data is that maltreatment is not treated as a unitary phenomenon (see also Bath & Haapala, 1993; Daro, 1988; Giovannoni, 1985); findings are presented that differentiate the outcome of a history of sexual abuse compared to physical abuse, as well as multiple abuse (both physical and sexual abuse) compared to no abuse. In addition, as Smith and Howard (1994) recommend, this chapter fills a research gap by longitudinally following adopted children who have a history of trauma from abuse.

RESULTS

Effects of Sexual Abuse

Quantitative Findings. Parents reported that 49.3% (N=35) of the children had no history of sexual abuse, 23.9% (N=17) of the children had a history of sexual abuse, and 26.8% (N=19) of the children were suspected to have been sexually abused prior to adoptive placements. The effects of reported history of sexual abuse were analyzed for behavior problems, attachment patterns, and family functioning. The effects of abuse over time in each of these three areas were also probed.

To examine the effects of child sexual abuse on behavior problems, the percent of children scoring in the clinical range on each of the behavior profiles of the Child Behavior Checklist was compared to the different categories of sexual abuse history. The clinical range consists of scores that serve as cutoff scores to differentiate between children referred for mental health services and "typical" children identified via representative sampling. Figure 5.1 presents the percent of children who score in the clinical range by sexual abuse history. The percent of children who scored in the clinical range was highest for children with a known or suspected history of sexual abuse and lowest for children with no history of sexual abuse for all behavior

Figure 5.1
Percent Scoring in Clinical Range of CBC
by Sexual Abuse History

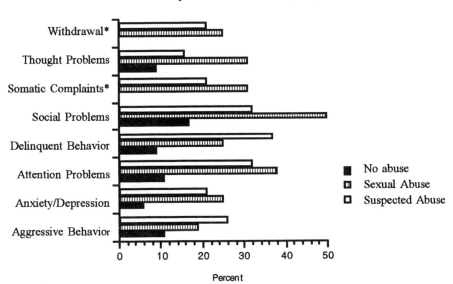

*Zero percent of children with no sexual abuse history scored in the clinical range

problems. Subsequent analysis explored patterns of behavior over time by sex abuse history. There was little fluctuation in these differences over time, suggesting that behavior problems are different depending on sex abuse history but do not alter over the course of 4 years depending on abuse history.

Sexual abuse history had a statistically significant effect on most variables measuring attachment. Both anxious attachment and avoidant attachment patterns were significantly higher for children with a known or suspected history of sexual abuse compared to children with no such history. The variables assessing getting along, trust, respect, and feeling close were significantly different, with the best relations reported for children with no abuse history and worst relations for children known or suspected to have been sexually abuse. Table 5.1 presents these findings.

Additional analysis explored patterns of attachment over time by sexual abuse history. There was little fluctuation in these differences over time, suggesting that these patterns of attachment are different depending on sex abuse history but do not alter over the course of 4 years depending on abuse history.

Sexual abuse history had no statistically significant effect on family adaptability or family cohesion. Table 5.2 presents categories of family functioning compared to sexual abuse history. Regarding adaptability, most parents (the modal category)

Table 5.1
Relationship Items by Sexual Abuse History

	% reporting very high		
	No Abuse	Sex Abuse	Sex Abuse Suspected
Get along with child*	72	53	49
Communication	46	29	41
Trust*	44	20	22
Respect*	61	32	33
Feel close to child*	73	41	57
Ambivalent* (mean)	2.4	4.4	3.9
Avoidant* (mean)	1.8	2.9	3.3

*p<.05

Table 5.2
Comparison of Family Functioning (Categories on FACES III)
by Sexual Abuse History

	Sexual Abuse		
	No Abuse	Sexual Abuse	Sexual Abuse Suspected
Family Adaptability (percents)			
Rigid	8.6	11.8	5.3
Structured	31.4	35.3	42.1
Flexible	20.0	23.5	31.6
Chaotic	40.0	29.4	21.1
Family Cohesion (percents)			
Disengaged	11.4	11.8	21.1
Separated	28.6	29.4	21.1
Connected	37.1	35.3	52.6
Enmeshed	22.9	23.5	5.3

parenting a child with no abuse history reported the family as chaotic, and most families parenting a child with a known or suspected sexual abuse history viewed the family as structured. Regarding cohesion, most parents viewed the family as connected for all 3 categories of sexual abuse history. There was little fluctuation in these differences over time by category of abuse, suggesting that family functioning does not differ depending on sex abuse, nor does it alter over the course of 4 years depending on abuse history.

Qualitative Findings. In addition to examining the quantitative data, family comments were analyzed. Only 3 families where the child had experienced known sexual abuse but had no physical abuse history made comments on the surveys. While each of the 3 cases in this category has a slightly different profile, some general themes are present. Some of the themes readily identified in the data reflect issues of trust, power/control, and anger (both expressed and suppressed), as well as the need for love and attention.

One case provides brief information in that the parent states that the child "didn't want to obey" and that "this child ran away at 14 1/2." Two issues seem to be at play in these data. The first issue seems to be the difficulty in successfully negotiating the parent/child relationship, while the second issue is literally the running-away behavior. Physically running away also may suggest that an emotional distancing was attempted as well. Thus, while the parent's comment that the child lacks a desire to "obey" seems to suggest an issue of anger or control, the physically running away could also be an expression of emotional distancing.

In another case, while the mother "expected a rotten child," she found that "she [the adopted daughter] is your basic kid that needs a lot of love." Still, the issue of emotional distancing is identified as an issue in their relationship, as the mother states, "She's really a good girl except for . . . not wanting me to get close to her." In this same vein, the parent recognizes that while her daughter "can be very loving and giving to others . . . her past has really put her in a shell." This emotional withdrawal may also be reflected in the mother's comment that "she [the daughter] spends too much time in her room alone."

Issues of power and control emerge as the mother states, "I have a hard time getting her to listen and not wanting to be the boss . . . she always wants to be in charge and to control everything and everyone." A related theme of anger is evident in the comment that the daughter "argues constantly and tries to make me [mother] feel wrong always."

In the last case, while lying and stealing are identified as concerns for the parents, so is their daughter's "need for attention from strangers." However, the daughter is also described as "very loving . . . a very happy girl . . . [and] very helpful to others." While the comments do not define a problem in terms of anger or withdrawal specifically, the need for attention from others, and a loving, happy, helpful nature, combined with a tendency toward lying and stealing, raise some question as to the degree to which negative emotions may have been suppressed or if the child is experiencing some attachment difficulty. More specifically, if this child does not behave in a manner that is loving and helpful, what is her perception of possible consequences? Is there some fear of being abandoned or abused if negative emotions are allowed to surface? While these questions cannot be directly answered from the data, these and the other issues outlined before parallel the framework generally used

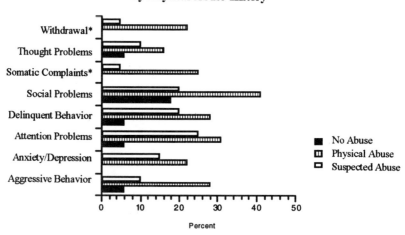

Figure 5.2
Percent Scoring in Clinical Range of CBC
by Physical Abuse History

*Zero percent of children with no physical abuse history scored in the clinical range

for understanding sexual abuse trauma (Finkelhor & Browne, 1985, 1986), as well as the findings of a previous study on the effects of sexual abuse on adoption outcome (Smith & Howard, 1994).

Effects of Physical Abuse

Quantitative Findings. Parents reported that 24.3% (N=17) of the children had no history of physical abuse, 47.1% (N=33) had a history of physical abuse, and 28.6% (N=20) were suspected to have been physically abused prior to adoptive placements.

Figure 5.2 presents the results on behavior, comparing the percent of children who score in the clinical range by physical abuse history. The percent of children who scored in the clinical range was highest for children with a history of physical abuse and lowest for children with no history of physical abuse. A greater percent of children with a history of suspected physical abuse scored in the clinical range compared to children with no physical abuse history although the percent was lower than for the children with a known history of physical abuse.

Subsequent analysis explored patterns of behavior over time by history of physical abuse. As with the results for sexual abuse, there was little fluctuation in these differences over time by abuse history. The findings suggest that behavior problems are different depending on physical abuse history but do not alter over the course of 4 years by category of abuse.

Qualitative Findings. The written comments add to the understanding of the behavior issues. The more severe problems are indicated by parents' comments such as:

Walter is a defiant child. He is not motivated by rewards or deterred by any punishments. He seems indifferent to consequences . . . his extreme impulsiveness which leads to stealing and then lies to cover up has now taken place at home, school and this month at a store. I fear he will be arrested. (physical abuse suspected, placed at age 5)

Temper tantrums are horrible . . . at times he's really fine behavior wise, but other times it is really horrible, defiant, destructive. (known physical abuse, placed at age 1)

The constant tension and her periodic tantrums/severe emotional displays our inability to handle it well. . . . Her willingness to inflict hurt and destruction upon people who don't give her what she wants. She can be very cruel and disruptive. (physical abuse suspected, placed at age 4)

There seem to be some other factors associated with these behavioral difficulties such as an attention deficit disorder (ADD) diagnosis, a fear of being abandoned, and an inability to trust.

Regarding ADD, the parents report the child's interest and ability to engage in social activities, on one hand, but impulsive and sometimes destructive behavior, on the other hand. It seems as though this dichotomy in behavior is frustrating and tiring for the parents. One parent states, "The lying, stealing and destructiveness of our 3 adopted children have become almost more than any married couple can stand." The issues of fear of abandonment and inability to trust are explored further in the next section on attachment.

Quantitative Findings. Physical abuse history had a statistically significant effect on most variables measuring attachment. Both anxious attachment and avoidant attachment patterns were significantly higher for children with a known or suspected history of physical abuse compared to children with no history. The variables assessing getting along, trust, respect, and feeling close were significantly different, with the best relations reported for children with no abuse history and worst relations for children known or suspected to have been physically abused. Table 5.3 presents these findings.

Additional analysis explored patterns of attachment over time by physical abuse history. As with the results for sexual abuse history, there was little fluctuation in these differences over time by category of abuse. The findings suggest that these patterns are different depending on physical abuse history but do not alter over the course of 4 years by physical abuse history.

Qualitative Findings. In further exploring the attachment issues by examining parents' written comments, the fear of abandonment seems to be a part of the parent/child relationship and in certain situations this fear can be pronounced. One case in particular illustrates this point. A physically abused child, Lima, placed at age 2 was adapting quite well to her new family environment until her adoptive father died

Table 5.3
Relationship Items by Physical Abuse History

	% reporting very high		
	No Abuse	Physical Abuse	Physical Abuse Suspected
Get along with child*	78	53	56
Communication#	48	34	43
Trust*	48	28	23
Respect*	68	42	28
Feel close to child*	78	56	53
Ambivalent* (mean)	2.3	3.9	3.2
Avoidant* (mean)	1.4	2.8	2.8

*p<.05, #p<.10

suddenly of a heart attack. In 1990 the adoptive mother's comments were positive, indicating that "nothing" was different from what was expected with regard to this adoption and that the most rewarding aspect for the mother has been "watching her [daughter] grow from an infant to a very intelligent and beautiful young lady." Furthermore, in 1990, the only concern expressed was "finances." The 1991 data, however, reflect this child's rising concerns of abandonment. The adoptive mother states, "Ever since my husband passed [away] she is afraid that someone else in the family will die too." From this point forward, Lima's behavior appears to deteriorate. In 1992 the adoptive mother states: "Things have really gone bad. Lima is not happy anymore and says she really hates me, but doesn't know why. . . . She gets pretty violent." The situation does not seem to have improved by 1993, as a concern noted by the adoptive mother is "the abusive language she [Lima] uses to me and other people." In light of her adoptive father's death, Lima's fears of abandonment do not seem to be irrational. Unfortunately, Lima's ensuing behaviors seem to reinforce this fear/belief as, according to the adoptive mother in 1992: "The other members of the family don't want me to keep her anymore . . . I am going to keep her as long as I can."

A similar pattern of behavior associated with a fear of abandonment can be seen in another case. In this particular case, of a child physically abused and placed at 1 year of age, the data are more explicit in establishing a connection between this fear and behavior problems. In 1990 the adoptive parent comments:

After court he commented no one could ever take him away, he has a real Mom and Dad now forever and ever. It's a relief to us knowing he's here to stay to. . . . Dealing with some behavior problems–temper tantrums are horrible, he has such an attachment to us--this comes and goes where he hates to be left at a sitter for example he's afraid we're not coming back.

In 1992, this fear is again noted by the adoptive parent:

We were hoping he would feel more secure than he does. He's afraid of losing us. With being foster parents the foster children remind him of things before his adoption, like leaving us weekends. He's very concerned about family members. When there is an illness he is very concerned about that person. (worried)

As in the previous case, the issue of illness seems to trigger worry or concern, not only about that person but perhaps more specifically about what the outcome of an illness could mean, that is, loss and abandonment if that person should die.

An additional attachment issue associated with physical abuse is the lack of trust. Three families in particular write about trust as an issue in inhibiting attachment between the adoptive parent and child. Furthermore, in each case, the adoptive parent also seems to associate this lack of trust with behaviors that are a source of conflict between the parent and child. One parent of a physically abused child who was placed at age 6 states: "I was not prepared for the turmoil that he would bring to our household or for how long it would last. I never thought that my relationship to one of my kids would be so difficult. Sometimes we're close, sometimes we're enemies." Another adoptive parent states quite clearly that:

Janie has never developed the trust and love for me that I hoped she would. She's quite independent and that's good to see but she has difficulty being part of a group. She can't be just one of the members, she has to be the center or else she is quite disruptive. Her younger brothers were both infants when they were adopted and have bonded much closer. Janie sees this and feels jealous about it, but to me it seems it's her own unwillingness to trust us that keeps her apart. (physical abuse suspected, child placed at age 4)

It would seem that Janie's inability to trust and respect her adoptive parents is associated, in the eyes of her adoptive parents, with "the constant tension and her periodic tantrums/severe emotional displays . . . also her need for control of others. . . [and] her willingness to inflict hurt and destruction upon people who don't give her what she wants."

While the data of a third case of a child suspected of having been physically abused and placed at age 10 indicate that the adoptive parent is the one who has difficulty trusting the adopted child, this lack of trust is attributed to untrustworthy behaviors of her daughter. In response to the question, What has been most difficult? the adoptive parent states, " Dealing with the lies and not trusting her like I would like." In addition, the adoptive parent indicates that the child is "not trustworthy at this point." In light of this comment, it would seem that the adoptive parent's difficulty in trusting is related to the child's untrustworthy behavior.

To balance the negative behaviors and attachment difficulties, of note in the data is the number of adoptive parents who have referred to the qualities of love, kindness, sensitivity, or ability of their child to have positive relationships with others. The data of 16 cases in this group reflect such remarks. In addition, 8 of the 16 were adoptive parents who also referred to moderate or more serious behavior problems in their adopted child. In the data of the remaining 8 cases, the adoptive parents remarked only on the positive qualities of their adopted son or daughter. The following quotes come from the data that reflect these more positive characteristics of the children as organized by degree of behavioral difficulties experienced by the family, from most difficult to purely positive.

[He] is a sweet, neat kid, very lovable child. He's learning ABC's, counting to 20, his address, phone no.--doing well. Loves the family and outside, very attached to his adoptive brothers. (physically abused, placed at age 1)

Jake is a very likable and witty boy who loves social activity. Because of this we have gotten to know more people in the community. (physical abuse suspected, placed at age 7)

She's a wonderful person who has come into our lives for us to know and watch grow . . . . Very intelligent, active, adventuresome, fearless, loves animals and is very good with them. [She] has very good morals [and a] concern for the whole world when her temper is under control. (physical abuse suspected, placed at age 4)

It is remarkable what a neat person Mark (as well as his siblings) [is] despite the very dramatic start he had in life. . . . He is outgoing, vivacious and tremendously optimistic. His intentions are always good and he is a perceptive child. He has an optimistic sensitivity to other people. These things can't be taught. (physical abuse suspected, placed at age 5)

She is a bubbling, energetic, very social girl--she's loving and giving. . . . She has been a warm, loving, kind and thoughtful daughter. (physical abuse suspected, placed at age 10)

Mia is very social, very likable, can charm the socks off of just about anyone. She is also generally responsible and reliable, active in school and outside activities, and fun to be around . . . [a] delightful conversationalist [and] makes friends easily. (physical abuse suspected, placed at age 6)

He has added lots of fun and joy to our family. . . . He is a lovable, likable little boy. (physical abuse suspected, placed at age 2)

She's a smart little girl, very willing to please, very loving . . . hangs in there through family problems. (physically abused, placed at age 6)

The love given and received has been great . . . very loving and trusting. (physically abused, placed at age 2)

He's such a neat boy. He is a joy to be around most of the time. (physically abused, placed at age 1)

She has brought great joy to the lives of all who know her. She brings love and laughter to all my time with her. (physically abused, placed at age 10)

Just having him around. His outgoing, loving personality . . . his friendliness towards others . . . good natured. (physically abused, placed at age 2)

She is wonderful. Alicia has brought so much love and joy into our lives, and I know secretly we are giving her the same . . . . She is very talented and very personable and friendly . . . wants to make others happy. (physical abuse suspected, placed as an infant)

Quantitative Findings. Finally, the effects of physical abuse history on family functioning were explored. Physical abuse history had no statistically significant effect on family adaptability or family cohesion. Table 5.4 presents categories of family functioning compared to physical abuse history. Regarding adaptability, most parents (the modal category) who adopted a child with no abuse or a child suspected to have been physically abused reported the family as chaotic. Most families parenting a child with a known physical abuse history viewed the family as structured. Regarding cohesion, most parents viewed the family as connected for children with no or a suspected physical abuse history. Most families who adopted a child with a known physical abuse history reported the family as separated or connected. There was little fluctuation in these differences over time by category of abuse, suggesting that family functioning does not differ depending on physical abuse history, nor does it alter over the course of 4 years depending on abuse history.

Table 5.4
Comparison of Family Functioning (Categories on FACES III)
by Physical Abuse History

	Physical Abuse		
	No Abuse	Physical Abuse	Physical Abuse Suspected
Family Adaptability (percents)			
Rigid	11.8	6.1	5.0
Structured	17.6	42.4	40.0
Flexible	23.5	33.3	10.0
Chaotic	47.1	18.2	45.0
Family Cohesion (percents)			
Disengaged	5.9	15.2	15.0
Separated	17.6	36.4	20.0
Connected	58.8	36.4	35.0
Enmeshed	17.6	12.1	30.0

Effects of Multiple Abuse (Physical and Sexual)

The final series of analysis is a subgroup analysis that examines the effects of both sexual and physical abuse. Combining results for the items assessing physical and sexual abuse, parents reported that 21.1% (N=15) of the children had no history of physical or sexual abuse and 19.7% (N=14) of the children had a history of both physical and sexual abuse prior to adoptive placements. With such small numbers, only the qualitative data are reported in detail. In general, analysis of the quantitative data is the same as for the data on physical and sexual abuse history. Children with a history of multiple abuse have significantly higher scores on the CBC for all behavior problem scales and demonstrate more attachment difficulties. Over time these effects remain the same. As with the findings for physical and sexual abuse, a history of multiple abuse has no effect on family functioning.

Drawing from written comments, children with multiple abuse generally suffer from low self-esteem, have difficulty trusting others, and demonstrate a wide range of behavioral problems that can include unpredictable and sometimes violent behavior. Although somewhat less outstanding at first glance, but no less significant, the theme of needing to please others or be helpful or needing attention from others emerges from the data. In fact, 11 of the cases that fall within this category of multiple abuse implicitly or explicitly express this theme of pleaser/helper.

Explicit comments made by several adoptive parents include the following:

So far this has been an easy adjustment. She is trying very hard to please us. (physically and sexually abused, placed at age 10)

Kit is a happy, outgoing, positive child who is generous, anxious to please and generally excited about life. (physically and sexually abused, placed as an infant)

Things have gone pretty well with Monica. She is a pretty, sensitive girl who wants to please everyone . . . always helps with house, washing anything. (physically and sexually abused, placed at age 10)

Very loving and affectionate, very caring and empathetic, good artist, wants to please. She loves me. (physical and sexual abuse suspected, placed at age 3)

She tries real hard to please. (physically abused, sexual abuse suspected, placed at age 9)

. . . very pleasant, willing and cooperative. (physical abused, sexual abuse suspected, placed at age 7)

While this last quotation is not phrased specifically as "wanting to please," the elements of "pleasant" and "cooperative" suggest behavior that is conforming, nonproblematic, and generally pleasing to adults. Somewhat more implicit are the following comments:

She's gentle . . . a good listener, respectful . . . thoughtful, quiet. (physically and sexually abused, placed at age 9)

She's thoughtful, warm. (physically and sexually abused, placed at age 8)

He is outgoing, extremely polite. He is very helpful when someone needs him. He is very loving, kind child very considerate. (physically abused, sexual abuse suspected, placed at age 6)

Loving-caring-gentleness-happy . . . friendly-sensitive-polite. (physical and sexual abuse suspected, placed at age 6)

One adoptive parent of a child physically abused also suspected to have been sexually abused who was placed at age 4 stated that her adopted daughter's "smile and (her) temperament" were a couple of the best things about her child. This parent also expressed concern about the fact that people might "take advantage of her [daughter's] easy going ways." Again, the implied message is that this girl has perhaps placed her needs second in order of priority to the needs or wants of others. This particular child's behavior is more noteworthy given the fact that the adoptive parent has also commented on the disruptive behavior of the daughter's siblings, who were also adopted by this family.

Given the background of abuse that these children have experienced, one might question the genuineness of this pleasing behavior in the sense that it would seem that an individual could not come through such experiences without some feelings of anger and rage. In essence, the question is, What other feelings or behaviors might be hiding behind this pleasant, helpful exterior? This question is given some validation in the data, as 1 adoptive parent acknowledges her concern about the fact that her daughter holds "her feelings inside at times" (physically and sexually abused, placed at age 9). In addition, this same adoptive parent notes the sense of "protection toward mom and dad" that this child demonstrates.

There could be a myriad of reasons for this pleasant exterior that could range from a sense of loyalty or need to protect the biological parent(s), to a fear of rejection if not well behaved, to a desire to be accepted and loved, to a fear of punishment, or even to a learned behavior that may have assisted in diffusing volatile situations in the (original) home environment. Whatever the motivation, the data seem to show that for a number of children, this behavior may be too difficult to maintain with any consistency. The outcome for these children seems to be a swing in mood or behavior from one extreme to another. As one parent notes, it is as if the child does not "recognize that he has control over his behaviors" (physical and sexual abuse suspected, placed at age 4). This particular child is described in the following manner: "Tries to please others, highly inquisitive and can learn easily and quickly; while also having poor impulse control. Gets upset, then gets angry, then out of control of himself."

This particular theme is clearly articulated in 5 other cases as the parents comment on their adopted children:

So sweet--cares about others--wants to be helpful--wants to please. . . . Mood swings--goes from very loving to very mean--pouty--very much a martyr--lack of self esteem. (sexually abused, physical abuse suspected, placed at age 4)

She is trying very hard and wants to please us. . . . She is pretty and can be loving. She is a wonderful person waiting to happen. . . . She is dishonest, destructive, vengeful, passive aggressive. She hurts people. (physically and sexually abused, placed at age 10)

We have a son who, for the most part, is very loving . . . his temper and learning to deal with it. He can really hurt someone because of his outbursts and not realizing what he's doing but he is sorry and apologizes afterward. He is nice to talk to when alone. (physically abused, suspected sexual abuse, placed at age 10)

Seeing the progress he has made. Seeing him fit into our family, make friends, do well in school. His expression of being happy to be part of our family. The unpredictability of his mood swings--having him go out of control, destroying property, threatening my life over seemingly small issues. Even though I realize this came from an inability to cope with his fears and past, I still have trouble trusting him. I feel the need to stay on top of things and be prepared to deal with a violent episode. (physical and sexual abuse suspected, placed at age 10)

Bernard's growth and understanding of himself and his love for me. . . . His anger and separation anxiety about his family. . . . [He] has a great personality [and] is honest.

Yet, the parent also notes concern about "anger and anger reactions" (physically and sexually abused child, placed at age 11). In essence, the mood and behavior of some of these children seem to cover both ends of the spectrum, from being loving and wanting to please to being angry and aggressive or out of control.

The anger and lack of control that some children seem to display are a combination that appears to be the most distressing to the adoptive parents. The data suggest a sense of fatigue or frustration on the part of the parent in response to these behaviors. One parent of a physically and sexually abused child placed at age 8 notes a concern about "the manner in which she [daughter] sets herself up to fail. She does not take direction and seems only to learn from the most traumatic personal experiences . . . the way she seems to set up adversarial relations between significant people in her life. Hating one so that she can get closer to the other. Then reversing that when it helps her particular situation." Regarding her role as a parent, the mother states that "the time and energy expenditure of parenting far exceeds what I thought it would be" and that "the referee-ing and continuous attention these children required was stressful for adults."

Comments from other adoptive parents reflecting distress in the face of angry or out-of- control behavior include the following:

Discipline--inability to reason with her and her lack of control over her own behavior. It has been difficult dealing with child's lack of responsibility--not being able to trust her to do what is expected. The learning situation and difficulty getting help from the school system have also been frustrating. Her habit of giving up if things are too hard. Running away, susceptible to suggestions of her peers. (physically and sexually abused, placed at age 7)

We expected him to adapt to us easier. He has had difficulty with stealing and honesty. We expected to get this in perspective right away. He is a compulsive liar. If he thinks no one is watching or won't get caught he'll steal or destroy property or light fires. (physically and sexually abused, placed at age 9)

His radical behavior changes and the physical abuse, he has hurt *everyone* (which required doctor visits). He needed help but all they [the agency] wanted to do was keep [him] in our home. I suffered a fractured sternum . . . . I had to threaten to kill him before they would place him. (physically abused, suspected sexual abuse, placed at age 7)

We expected things to be difficult but for about 3 years felt problems were solvable--As child grew older the acting out became more grown up, increased violence toward adoptive family. We did not realize we would be held responsible for birth parents and foster parents actions, by the child . . . . The cost to our family has been great. We would not have adopted these problems. We love our son! Love is not enough. (physically and sexually abused, placed at age 7)

The issue of anger and aggression is somewhat complex in that, as previously suggested, it is not always a straightforward or situationally related emotion. Generally, the anger is a more pervasive, underlying emotion that many of the children express in terms of defiance toward those in authority. Though not explicit, the data for one case suggest that the child is physically abusive toward his parents and that an adolescent treatment center was not able to contain his destructive behavior. In this particular case, it would seem that authority has little or no effect on the management of this child's behavior.

The data on 3 additional cases are more conclusive in their identification of defiance toward authority. The parents' comments are as follows:

The school problems and Pat's lack of motivation and acting out around school issues. . . . lack of respect for teacher and some peer conflicts. (physically and sexually abused, placed at age 7)

The continued signs in her that show her negative self-esteem, inability to have positive relationships with others, and her defiance against authority. (physically and sexually abused, placed at age 8)

The child has a total disregard for the parent--child relationship. She wants to do just whatever she pleases (most of the time). . . . In foster placement, discipline problems, running away . . . my biggest concern is with the fact that she listens to no one in authority. (physically abused, sexual abuse suspected, placed at age 7)

For other children, there seems to be a clearer link between anger and the child's history of abuse or issues pertaining to the relationship with the biological families. In several cases, the data suggest that the adoptive families experience difficulty with their adopted son or daughter's behavior following the child's contact with his or her biological family:

Child harder to handle after visits [with biological mother and/or father]. (physically abused, sexual abuse suspected, placed at age 4)

Niles was too young to have bonded with his siblings so he doesn't respond as they do. He really doesn't understand who they are. He has some negative reactions--recurrence of nightmares--insecurity. (physical and sexual abuse suspected, placed as an infant)

We try to get the . . . children together at least once a year. It is important for them to see that each is okay and doing well. We do find that after visits, the children act out past behavior and have trouble in school. (physically and sexually abused, placed at age 6)

All will be invited to our home . . . Ramona appears to have little reaction. Her twin on the other hand, reflects very negative behaviors afterward. (physical and sexual abuse suspected, placed at age 7)

To this point, pleasing and angry/acting out behavior as it relates to the adopted child's abusive background has been identified. One other key mode of interacting or coping with the world emerges from the data, namely, withdrawal or denial. In one case this withdrawal is severe to the point of suggesting a diagnosis of dissociative disorder. In this particular case, the child has demonstrated "almost constant difficult behavior" (physical and sexual abuse suspected, placed at age 4). While the family felt that the adoption worker was "very honest in making us aware of the possible persistent emotional problems . . . the major difficulty has been the fact that there was abuse in his background that the social workers were not aware of." Through therapy it was revealed that the child has sustained severe abuse resulting in a "dissociative disorder." In another case, the parent expresses positive feelings with regard to "watching her [daughter] overcome fears and low self-esteem when those things are removed--then comes this bubbly personality and happy spirit" (physically and sexually abused, placed at age 8). However, regardless of this "happy" attitude, the adoptive parent also notes that her daughter has "never accepted that she was abused." In a third case, the adoptive parent notes that this withdrawal or denial is seen more as "an avoidance of reality when she [daughter] is stressed" (physical and sexual abuse suspected, placed at age 3). The two remaining cases refer to the fact that the child may, at times, "hold feelings inside" and that "problems have put her [the daughter] in a shell."

Throughout the data, in addition to the themes of anger/aggression, defiance, pleasing behavior, and withdrawal/denial or avoidance of reality, there is an associated dimension of low self-esteem. In other words, many adoptive parents have also noted low self-esteem as an issue in conjunction with one of the aforementioned issues. Such comments by parents are noted in the following quotes:

The continued signs in her that show her negative self-esteem, inability to have positive relationships with others, and her defiance of authority. (physically and sexually abused, placed at age 8)

Watching her overcome fears and low self-esteem. (physically and sexually abused, placed at age 8)

Mood swings--goes from very loving to very pouty--very much a martyr--lack of self-esteem. (sexually abused, physical abuse suspected, placed at age 4)

Self discipline in cleaning her room and personal hygiene--low self-esteem--thinks she doesn't have many friends--she also likes to be very bossy. (physically and sexually abused, placed at age 3)

[I am] concerned about her training from birth mom to gain self-esteem by being sexually active. (physically and sexually abused, placed at age 9)

Her lack of motivation, low self-esteem. I hope she can develop skills for employment in a field she likes. (physically and sexually abused, placed at age 8)

Seeing her security and self confidence grow. (physically abused, sexual abuse suspected, placed at age 8)

Finally, while identified in only two cases, the theme of sensitivity to vulnerable groups (i.e., the elderly, babies, and small animals) is noteworthy. This theme is of interest because it contrasts with the prevalent behaviors and emotions that seem to be obstacles to establishing close, trusting relationships with other people. One of the cases of a child placed at age 8 who was physically abused and suspected to have been sexually abused has been previously mentioned in relation to the child's inability to take direction and her tendency to set up adversarial relationships between significant people in her life. The adoptive parent also notes her daughter's "kindness to elderly, handicapped [and] babies" and her "love of animals . . . and children." In the second case of a child placed at age 6 who was physically and sexually abused, in reference to their adopted daughter, the parent states: "She loves to dress nice and is very clean about herself. She is overly loving and caring to others, especially to smaller children and older people."

SUMMARY OF MAJOR FINDINGS

Children who have been physically, sexually, or multiply abused have more behavior problems and attachment difficulties than nonabused children. Family functioning does not appear to be affected by abuse history. The findings on attachment and behavior are consistent with previous research. Of course, it cannot be concluded from the data that the abuse caused these difficulties. The only conclusion that can be made is that an abuse history is associated with more behavior problems and more attachment difficulties. While these differences exist, over time there seems to be little change in behavior or patterns of attachment depending on preadoptive abuse history. Parents' comments provide more details about the stresses they encounter in parenting the children with traumatic preadoptive histories.

6

Social Support and the Adoptive Family

THE ECOLOGICAL PERSPECTIVE

All families live and interact with their environment. Recognizing the role the environment (i.e., neighborhood, community, city, county) can play has been called the ecological perspective. This perspective is unique because it does not focus on the internal dynamics of a family or individual; rather, the ecological perspective examines the way that families affect and respond to their environment, as well as how the environment affects families. This perspective recognizes that understanding the social environment of families is a critical component in understanding the overall functioning of the family as a complex social system (Hartman & Laird, 1983; Pilisuk & Parks, 1983). As part of the ecological perspective, it is important to understand social networks, social support, and social support networks.

A social network is the "web of interpersonal relations that tie the individual together with others" (Garbarino, 1983, p. 19). It means those people and organizations that provide social interaction with the family. Social support is a perceived event, a result of the action of others. Supportive behaviors include approval, help, guidance, kindness, emotional help, information, and concrete aid. It is those behaviors that an individual or family perceives as helping it or influencing its life. A social support network is a set of interconnected relationships that provide durable patterns of interaction and interpersonal relations; it is a relationship structure where people can make demands and request help (Garbarino, 1983, p. 4). It generally comprises those people in the life of a family who help it cope with everyday issues. It often includes the extended family, friends, neighbors, colleagues, and service providers on which families rely in their day-to-day lives. Caplan (1974) indicates that support systems play a significant role in maintaining physical and psychological health.

Social support may be continual as provided within enduring relationships, or intermittent and short-term in the event of an acute need or crisis. That is, social support can be found in relationships that are ongoing, such as the relationships that many families have with extended family members or long-term friends. In addition, social support can be developed to meet a need that just develops and can be obtained from relationships that are new and time-limited. The latter relationships likely consist of three elements: (1) the support person "helps the individual to mobilize his/her psychological resources and master emotional burdens"; (2) they share his or her tasks; and (3) they provide him or her with "extra supplies of money, materials, tools, skills, and cognitive guidance to improve his/her handling of a situation" (Caplan, 1974, p. 6). The crisis-support relationship usually is dissolved after the crisis is over. However, sometimes families incorporate into their family life the person who provided the short-term help and go on to develop a longer-term relationship with that person or persons.

Social support is provided on two levels. First, there is the informal or natural system. This support develops spontaneously from family, friends, work associates, school colleagues, or neighbors. When people need help, the first sources of assistance are usually those in the interpersonal or informal networks (Gottlieb, 1988). Second, there is the formal system. This is the support received from social workers, doctors, lawyers, clergy, and other professionals (Caplan, 1974; Maguire, 1991). This is the system that families are more reluctant to involve. Even in the formal system, there is a hierarchy in the decision making of many families. Usually, they contact their clergy person before they venture into other elements of the formal system of support.

Caplan (1974, pp. 13-15) describes how people seek out formal helpers to intermittently augment natural supports when out-of-the-ordinary challenges or problems arise. For example, people with an illness or who are exposed to a personal or family predicament have a tendency to seek guidance from somebody who has had similar experiences and can tell what to expect as well as what options have helped in dealing with the burdens and challenges. When people experience difficulties, it is not unusual for them to combine formal and informal resources in their problem-solving endeavors to assist them in their adjustment. Thus, both the informal and formal systems can be part of a family's social support network. Sources of support can allow families to successfully navigate the difficulties they encounter.

THE VALUE OF SOCIAL SUPPORT

Social support system theory proposes that the ways people believe, act, and feel are affected by the people with whom they are interconnected in various ways. According to Maguire (1991), social support or an individual's social support network provides five resources. First, social support can provide a sense of self. Family and individual identity is shaped and reinforced by the people who are part of one's life. When a person challenges who the family is, sometimes the family or individual excludes that person from their lives. In other instances, the challenging helps families or individuals redefine who they are and the changes they made. Individuals and families learn and relearn about themselves through involvement with a supportive social system. Adoptive families must form a new sense of self when a child or children enter the family through adoption. Social support can help families as they define who they are as an adoptive family.

Second, social support can provide encouragement and positive feedback. A positive social support system provides people with feedback that they have worth and are valued. Adoptive families have many struggles as they attempt to integrate children into the new family. When they feel overburdened or hopeless, support systems can provide the reassurance and sense of hope that families need.

Third, social support gives protection against stress. As outlined in Chapter 1, adoptive families encounter unique stressors in the formation and maintenance of their family. Families and individuals with strong social supports handle stressors that occur in daily living more successfully (Gore, 1981; House, 1981; Caplan, 1974; Pearson, 1990). Feeling supported and cared about appears to decrease or buffer the negative effects of stressful life events. The absence of support or threatening or negative forces can present environmental risks to a family (Garbarino, 1983).

Fourth, social support contributes knowledge, skills, and resources to the adoptive family. Froland (1979) suggests that social support systems can help a family in defining a problem, in seeking the appropriate help through the informal system of referral, in buffering the stress, and in enhancing the effects of professional intervention by providing support before, during, and after professional assistance.

Fifth, support systems provide socialization opportunities. Some families have poorly developed social skills, or the social skills that were appropriate before an adopted child entered the family no longer are functional. Others may experience a temporary setback as a result of the adoption and the difficulties experienced in the adoption. For adoptive families, the uniqueness of their situation may leave them feeling isolated. With the lack of appropriate role models of what an adoptive parent is supposed to be like, they may feel lost. Interaction with others can reduce isolation and give families a forum for discussing the issues they face with others in similar situations. If the social system includes involvement with other adoptive parents, they have a forum for mutual sharing of issues they face that are similar.

SOCIAL SUPPORT SYSTEM INTERVENTIONS

Social support systems provide emotional support and nurturance, reinforcement (or punishment) for behavior, guidance, and access to resources such as information and tangible aid (Tracy & Whittaker, 1990; Gore, 1981; Whittaker & Garbarino, 1983). Social support system interventions can be used to minimize the effects of adverse social conditions and life stresses. Social support interventions can be of two types. First, intervention can focus on changing the structure of the social support network. For example, increasing the size of the network or changing the composition of the network would be structural interventions. Second, intervention can focus on changing the functional quality of social network relationships. For example, increasing the types of support in specific areas or increasing reciprocity in the social network relations would be functional interventions. The practice of increasing social support networks seems particularly pertinent in rural communities where there are limited professional resources available to deal with the range of psychosocial problems families encounter.

Maguire (1991) notes that social support system interventions reflect the value premise that family, friends, and informal sources of support are preferable to forms of therapy that do not include them. He suggests that positive outcomes are sustained because the supports become an ongoing part of the client's social system. This approach encourages families' awareness of their existing social network upon which they can call. Interventions include, among other techniques, the use of support groups and self-help groups (Maguire, 1991).

There is a difference between self-help groups and support groups. Generally, references to self-help groups specify no trained mental health professional as the leader (Ramsey, 1992). Leadership evolves from among those sharing the problem or concern (Maguire, 1991). Self-help groups for families may be formed for any number of reasons; whatever the goals, they provide social interaction and generally some degree of support for families. The members form bonds based on mutual identification and a shared problem or concern. The groups enable parents to decrease isolation, vent their feelings, and receive advice from other parents. Difficulties such as sibling rivalry, issues with grandparents, overprotectiveness, disagreements between parents regarding child rearing and general child development concerns are typical topics. Parents share similar experiences that may be painful or stressful. While parents acknowledge the value of information and support, they also appreciate the normalization of problems gained through group participation with other parents struggling with the same issues (Louv, 1993).

In contrast to self-help groups, support groups include professionals as leaders, facilitators, or consultants. Support groups may be developed for specific situations or for specific populations. Weiss (1976, cited in Maguire, 1991) discussed the social support needs of people in transitional states. Sometimes, parents find that their situations are unshared by intimate friends and family and that the problems they are attempting to cope with are different from those shared by their usual support community. To reduce their feelings or marginality and isolation, he suggests they need to find a temporary community of others "in the same situation, for whom their experiences will have meaning and who can fully accept them."

As a specific example, Karoloff and Friesen (1991) describe support groups for parents of children with emotional disorders. They note that parents of children with emotional disorders may feel guilty if they believe they caused or in some way contribute to the problem and may feel embarrassed or ashamed of their child's difficulties. Friends, relatives and professionals may blame them for the child's condition or parents may fear being blamed. In addition, parents may be frustrated by the lack of appropriate, available services in their attempts to plan for the educational and therapeutic needs of their children. Respite care, financial assistance, transportation, and access to recreational opportunities are among the services that may be difficult to locate. Support groups for these families can serve the function of providing information, parent-to-parent support, and advocacy for better services. These groups may be formally affiliated with an organization (school, agency, and so on) or more informal meetings of a small number of family members who share similar concerns.

Parent-to-parent support groups are intended to perform the important function of helping parents cope with the stresses of raising their child (Phillips, 1990). They can provide emotional reinforcement as well as a forum for sharing first-hand experience and information. They also can afford them opportunities for collective advocacy on behalf of their children. Groups for parents with chronically ill children function on the premise that parents who are caring for a child with similar needs or problems can share experiences and feelings that will help them to gain insights into their shared difficulties. The assumption is that interaction with families facing a similar crisis is therapeutic. Friendships, shared information, practical assistance, and advocacy activities are often outcomes of these groups.

THE ADOPTIVE FAMILY AND SOCIAL SUPPORT

Joining a family through adoption is a process that lasts a lifetime. Initially, the primary task of the adoptive family of a special needs child is family integration. Family integration means that the adopted child and the adoptive family assimilate each other's preadoptive experiences and change to develop a third family system, much like the experiences of blended families (Carter & McGoldrick, 1988).

This is a stressful process. However, it is important to recognize that stress occurs in all families, sometimes due to normative events such as a developmental change in an individual and other times from nonnormative events such as the hospitalization of a family member (McCubbin & Patterson, 1982). The extreme continuum of stress is crisis. Crisis occurs in a family when existing resources or coping skills are not sufficient to meet current demands and is characterized by family disorganization or disruptiveness (Patterson, 1988).

Whether an event in the life of the family is stressful or crisis-producing depends on the balance of stressors, coping skills, and resources in the family system. Resources include social support, which consists of emotional support (communication that one is loved, valued, and cared about) and interpersonal networks of people (Pearlin & Schooler, 1982); informational support (advice, suggestions and appraisals); and instrumental support, such as aid of any kind, including money, time, labor, respite (see Patterson, 1988, p. 217). Involvement with formal (e.g., professional service providers) and informal support systems (e.g., adoptive parents' support group) can provide more energy to the family system. Social support can strengthen the family and can buffer family stress; it is often viewed as a significant factor in promoting success in adoption (Nelson, 1985; Partridge, Hornby, & McDonald, 1986; Barth & Berry, 1988; Groze & Rosenthal, 1991a).

While social support is widely acknowledged by adoption researchers and practitioners, little detail is known about social support networks of adoptive families. The following analysis was designed to probe the issue of social support in adoptive families.

METHODOLOGY FOR EXAMINING SOCIAL SUPPORT

Besides yearly surveys, during the last year of the study, families were asked to participate in interviews to explore social support. Forty-four of the 71 families (62%) participated in the interviews. As part of the interview, families completed a social network map (see Chapter 2). The family was asked as a group to complete the social network map rather than completing a map for each member of the family. The results of these interviews and selected information about social support over the 4 years are presented here.

Social Network Characteristics

Network Size and Composition. The social network map allows for naming up to 15 individuals who are most important in the social network. Families reported from 1 to 14 people who were part of their social network. On average, families report 6.8 people; the median and mode were 6 people.

There are 7 domains for each family's network: (1) *household* (people with whom they live); (2) *other family*/relatives; (3) other *friends*; (4) people from *work/school*; (5) people from clubs, *organizations*, or religious groups; (6) *neighbors*; and (7) agencies or other formal service providers (*professionals*). As demonstrated from Figure 6.1, these adoptive families most often report other family members or relatives as forming the biggest percent of their social network (26.2%). Professionals make up 22.4% of the network. Individuals from clubs/organizations/church make up 13.9% of the network. Connections were about equal to individuals from work/school (12.6%) and other friends (12.2%). Neighbors (8.2%) and members inside the household (2.7%) were reported least often in the network map. It is interesting the degree that families rely on professionals; this finding is consistent with previous research about the overrepresentative of adopted children in more formal services. The explanation offered is that adoptive families, because of their extensive involvement with professionals during the home study and following the placement of an adopted child, have less of a stigma toward professional services and are more likely to turn to them when difficulties are encountered. For these families that certainly seems true.

Frequency of Contact. Most families report daily (21.9%) or weekly (30.5%) contact with some member of the network either by phone or in person. Families have daily contact most often with members of their household (88%), individuals from work or school (58%), and neighbors (52%). Weekly contact is most often with other friends (49%). Most families report that other family members are seen only a few times a year (39%), although 22% see them monthly, 27% see them weekly, and about 10% see them daily. Equal percents of families (29%) report seeing professionals monthly to several times a year although one-fifth (20%) report weekly contact.

Figure 6.1
Sources of Social Support

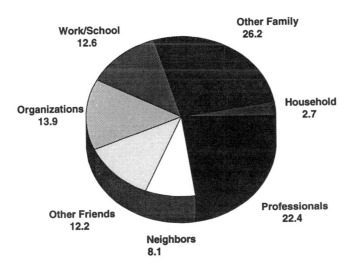

Stability of Network Relationships. The length of time people have been in the network is used as an indicator of the stability of the relationship (Tracy, 1990). Most individuals were reported to have been in the network for more than 5 years (69%), suggesting that most of these relationships are very stable. Only a few (8.8%) of the relationships are less than a year in duration. The relationships that are less than a year old are those from work or school and those from clubs, organizations, or religious groups.

Types and Sources of Social Support. A second function of the network map was to assess emotional support, concrete assistance, and information or advice and which members of the network provide such support. Forty-five percent of network members were perceived almost always available to provide concrete support, 65% were almost always available for emotional support, and 37% were almost always available for information and advice. Table 6.1 presents the different types of support for each domain. There is a statistically significant relationship between degree of concrete support and domain, and degree of information and domain. Adoptive families are significantly more likely to get concrete support from within the household (87.5%). They are also significantly more likely to get information or advice both from within the household (50%) and from professionals (61%).

Table 6.1
Types of Social Support by Domain (percent reporting almost always)

	Concrete Support	Emotional Support	Information or Advice*
Household	87.5%	87.5%	50.0%
Other Family	44.7%	63.6%	27.3%
Work/School	44.4%	56.8%	27.0%
Organizations	31.7%	63.4%	36.6%
Friends	54.3%	82.9%	37.1%
Neighbors	25.0%	50.0%	8.3%
Professionals	48.5%	63.6%	60.6%

*$p<.05$

Reciprocity. The vast majority (67%) of network relationships were perceived to be reciprocal. One hundred percent of household relations, 94% relations with friends, 78% of relations with people from groups/organizations/church, 76% of relations with other family members, 78% of relations with neighbors, and 69% of relations with people from school/work were seen as reciprocal. The least reciprocity was with relations with professionals, where most of the help comes from the professional to the family (74%).

Closeness. Families were asked how close they were to each person in the network. About 43% were perceived as very close, and 42% were perceived as sort of close. Closest relations were reported for people inside the household (88%), other family members (65%), and other friends (67%). People from work/school (57%), clubs/organizations/church (46%), neighbors (67%) and professionals (50%) were more often reported as sort of close.

Critiques. The social network map also identifies potential sources of stress by asking who is critical in a negative or demanding way. A minority of network members were reported as almost always critical (5.4%). A critique was most often from other family members when it did occur, although some criticism was also reported from individuals at work/school. Overall, however, the map suggests that there are more resources than sources of criticism in the network members identified by the family as part of their social network.

Adoption Services

During the first year, families were asked about adoption services. Regarding meeting with the adoption worker, most families (32%) reported meeting one to three times after placement, and most (70%) reported no meetings after finalization. The vast majority of parents (81%) thought the number of visits was adequate. Most families (63%) report that they received the right amount of information about their child, although a significant minority (37%) reported they did not get enough information. Most families reported the information received about their adopted child or children to be accurate (63%) or mostly accurate (27%). Overall, 60% of the families evaluate adoption services as very helpful, 26% reported them somewhat helpful, and 15% reported them not helpful.

Involvement with Individual and Family Therapy

In addition to gathering social network data and adoption service information, families were asked about their involvement with individual and family therapy. Figure 6.2 presents therapy service involvement over time. In general, there is an increase in participation in both individual and family therapy. During year 1, approximately 40% of the children participated in individual therapy, and during subsequent years this increased to 47%, 54%, and 58% of the children. About 30%

Figure 6.2
Formal Service Involvement over Time

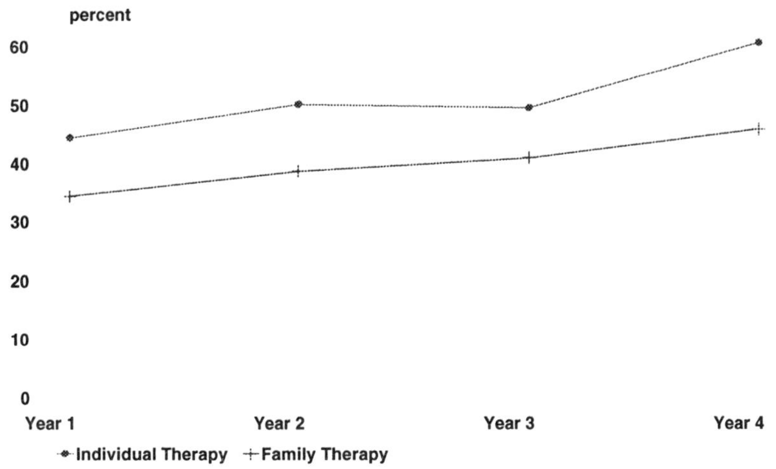

percent reporting participating

of the families in year 1 participated in family therapy, compared to 36% in year 2, 38% in year 3 and 43% in year 4. Families generally evaluate services positively. Over 80% of families report that therapy services are somewhat or very helpful, and this percent remained fairly consistent over the 4 years of the study.

This increase in formal service participation may be due to several factors. First, several postlegal adoption service grants were awarded throughout the state over this 4-year period, making adoption-sensitive services more available in some areas of the state. Second, over time a significant number of children approach adolescence. Adolescence, regardless of adoption status, can be problematic for some children. Parents may have responded by increasing their participation in services.

Support Groups

In addition to examining social support and formal service involvement, specific information about support groups was gathered. During the first year, about one-fourth (24.3%) of the families report support group attendance. This increased to about one-third of the families during year 2 (32.4%) and year 3 (31.3%). In year 4, this decreased to about one-fourth (25.4%). During the last year of the study, families were asked which family members attend support groups and the effect of support groups. Table 6.2 presents the results of this analysis. Most parents and their children did not attend support groups. For those who did, the majority found them to be of value. However, when asked about service needs, about 36% of respondents identified parent support groups as needed. While a geographical analysis is not possible, it may be that the parents who wanted support groups were in areas of the state where these groups were not easily available.

No relationship was found between support group attendance and the following: age of the child at time of the study, race of the child, race of the parent, marital status of parent, age of parent, and education of parent. The relationship between age of the child at placement and support group attendance approached significance ($t = 1.81$, $p = .08$), with parents who adopted older children (mean age = 6.1) reporting they attend parent support groups more often compared to parents who adopted younger children (mean age = 4.3). Children who were older at placement (mean=7.1) were more likely to be in a support group ($t = 2.37$, $p = .02$) compared to children adopted when younger (mean = 4.3). Parents with higher incomes were significantly more likely to attend support groups ($t = 2.10$, $p = .04$). Parents who had children who were reported to have more total problems were more likely to be attending support groups (attending mean = 56.4, not attending mean = 38.4, $t = 2.06$, $p = .04$). This suggests that support groups may be used by parents who are experiencing more difficulties in child behavior.

Table 6.2
Information on Support Groups

Child Attends Support Group	Yes	14.1%
	No	85.9%
Effect of Group on Child	Mostly good	38.5%
	Some good	23.1%
	Not much effect	30.8%
	More harm than good	7.7%
Which Parent Attends Support Group	One parent	46.7%
	Both parents	53.3%
Effect of Group on Family	Mostly good	66.7%
	Some good	14.3%
	Not much effect	19.0%

Social Contact with Other Adoptive Families

During the first year about 44% of the families had social contact with other adoptive families. This increased to 51% during year 2 and decreased to 46% by year 4 (this information was not collected during year 3). During year 1, most families (37%) reported seeing other families every 2 to 3 months. About 29% had monthly contact, 14% had weekly contact, 11% had yearly contact, and 9% had daily contact.
During year 2, most families (32%) had yearly contact with other families. About 30% had monthly contact, 23% saw other families every 2 to 3 months, 11% had weekly contact, and only 5% had daily contact. Over 90% of families report this contact as very or somewhat helpful during the first year, and this percent increased to 100% during year 2 and 97% in year 3.

Support for the Adoption

Families were asked about support for the adoption from relatives, spouse's relatives, and friends during years 1, 2 and 3. Table 6.3 presents parent perceptions of the support. Most families receive a great deal of support for the adoption from relatives, spouse's relatives and friends. Even though there are some changes between categories of support, these changes are not statistically significant. Thus, families receive a great deal of support from families and friends for the adoption, and this support is consistently high over time.

Table 6.3
Support for the Adoptive Placement over Time

	Year 1	Year 2	Year 3
Relatives Approve of the Adoption			
Yes, very much	70.4%	67.6%	64.8%
Somewhat	26.8%	25.4%	33.8%
No	2.8%	7.0%	1.4%
Spouse's Relatives Approve of the Adoption			
Yes, very much	63.3%	61.3%	56.7%
Somewhat	28.3%	30.6%	38.3%
No	8.8%	8.1%	5.0%
Friends Approve of the Adoption			
Yes, very much	85.9%	80.3%	76.8%
Somewhat	14.1%	15.5%	17.4%
No	0%	4.2%	5.8%

SOCIAL SUPPORT AND ADOPTION OUTCOMES

The relationship between various dimensions of the social support network and adoption outcomes was explored. Included in the exploration of outcomes were perceptions about parent/child relations, changes in parent-child relations over the 4-year period, the impact of the adoption, changes in how the parent viewed the impact perceptions of adoption, how often the parent thought of ending the adoptive placement, whether the parent would adopt again, and whether the parent would recommend adoption to others. Only significant findings are reported and should be viewed with caution, given the skewed data (most outcomes are very positive) and the small number of cases in bivariate and multivariate analysis.

The only parent who frequently thought of ending the adoptive placement was the lone parent who reported she hardly ever received emotional support (chi square=11.7, p=.02). There was also a significant relationship between emotional support and impact of the adoption at year 4 (chi-square=13.9, p=.03); families with greater emotional support reported more positive outcomes than families with less emotional support. For example, 50% of families who hardly ever received emotional support reported the impact of the adoption to be very positive, compared to 62.5% of families who sometimes got emotional support and 88.9% of the families who almost always got emotional support. There was also a significant relationship between emotional support and parent/child communication at year 4 (chi-square=16.8, p=.01); families with greater emotional support reported more positive communication than families with less emotional support. For example, 0% of families who hardly ever received emotional support reported the communication to be very positive, compared to 25.0% of families who sometimes got emotional support and 40.7% of the families who almost always got emotional support. There was also a significant relationship between emotional support and feeling close to the child at year 4 (chi-square=13.1, p=.01); families with greater emotional support reported closer relations than families with less emotional support. For example, 50% of families who hardly ever received emotional support reported feeling very close, compared to 62.5% of families who sometimes got emotional support and 70.4% of the families who almost always got emotional support. The same result approaches significance (chi-square=9.1, p=.06) for information/advice and feeling close.

GAPS IN SERVICES

The last area probed was the gaps in services or identification of service needs. Table 6.4 presents the results of this analysis. Several service needs stand out. About one-third of the families identified financial support as a needed service, and one-fourth identified routine medical and dental care as well as a support group for the adopted child as a need. In addition, one-fifth of families identified a support group for the parent, case management, counseling around adoption issues, and educational services as unmet needs.

SUMMARY

The families in this study identified and used both formal and informal sources of social support. Their involvement with formal support services (individual child therapy and family therapy) increased throughout the 4 years of the study. Informal support such as a support group for adoptive parents was not used very often, although those who did attend found it to be very helpful. Families perceive a great deal of support for the adoption from families and friends, and this support remained consistently high over time.

It is noteworthy that the families demonstrated a high rate of involvement with, and appreciation for, professional service providers. Professionals were the domain most frequently relied on for information and advice and were just as likely to be a source of emotional support as were family members outside the household and people from other organizations.

Considering the evidence that social support is a resource with powerful potential for the prevention and remediation of a wide range of biopsychosocial difficulties, social support intervention needs to be an integral part of social work practice (Pearson, 1990). A social worker can play a significant role in facilitating both the informal support system of family, friends, and neighbors as well as support groups such as the adoption parent support group (Garbarino, 1983). In many ways, intervention that builds on the networks that exist in the lives of adoptive families is

Table 6.4
Identification of Service Needs

	%	(n)
Respite Care	15.5	(11)
Special Day Care Services	4.2	(3)
Regular Day Care Services	7.0	(5)
Babysitting or Day Care (in home)	15.5	(11)
Homemaker or Housekeeping Services	4.2	(3)
Home Health or Nursing Care for Child	3.7	(2)
Adoptive Parent Support Group	21.1	(15)
Support Group for Adopted Child	25.4	(18)
Informal Contact with Other Adoptive Parents Informal Contact for Child with Other Adoptive Children	11.3	(8)
Social Worker's Help in Locating and Coordinating Services	15.5	(11)
Adoption Financial Subsidy	22.5	(16)
Other Financial Supports	35.2	(25)
Help or Counseling Concerning Issues Have to do with Adoption	33.8	(24)
Help or Counseling Regarding Parenting Skills	21.1	(15)
Help or Counseling about Child Development	16.7	(8)
Help or Counseling in Planning for Child's Future	8.5	(6)
Family Counseling/Therapy	16.9	(12)
Individual Counseling/Therapy for Child	16.9	(12)
Counseling to Prevent Out-of-Home Placement	14.1	(10)
Short-term "Shelter" Placement	4.2	(3)
Foster, Group or Residential Placement	4.2	(3)
Psychiatric Hospitalization	4.2	(3)
Psychological Evaluation Services	5.6	(4)
Educational Testing, Assessment or Planning	15.5	(11)
Specialized Educational Curriculum	21.1	(15)
Tutoring	16.9	(12)
Speech Therapy	16.9	(12)
Physical or Occupational Therapy	16.9	(12)
Routine Medical Care	12.7	(9)
Specialized Medical Care	26.8	(19)
Dental Care	2.8	(2)
Legal Services	26.8	(19)
	9.9	(7)

empowering and can facilitate a family-based perspective in adoption services. A family-based perspective in adoption would put the family in control of deciding who is involved in helping a family in mastering a difficulty. A family-based perspective recognizes that it is important to strengthen and work collaboratively with the informal helping resources already a part of the life of many adoptive families. This approach is also more culturally sensitive because it focuses on the natural social networks of Thus, any assessment of adoptive families should include evaluating the strengths and limitations of a family's social environment and the impact that environment has on the family. Visually displaying the information, such as with the use of ecomaps and social network maps, allows the adoptive family the opportunity to learn more about their own networks. By engaging the family in actively assessing their network, they can generate potential options for change and potential resources for meeting more of their needs in their existing network (Tracy, 1990).

Empowering families by building social support networks as part of an intervention strategy can enhance child development by providing emotional and material support as well as role models (Whittaker, 1983b; Cochran & Brassard, 1979). Whittaker (1983b) also suggested that this intervention is less restrictive and intrusive than other methods of affecting families. While no substitute for professional services, they can be an untapped resource for promoting stability in the life of adoptive families and one sector in a system of adoption services.

Social support networks may augment, complement, or serve as an alternative to, professional services in those communities where professional services do not exist, such as rural communities (Whittaker, 1983a, p. 29). For Whittaker (1983a), the essence of social work practice is to both build more supportive, helpful, and nurturing environments for clients and increase a client's competence in dealing with the environment (p. 36). For adoption services, this approach makes good practical, as well as clinical, sense. Many adoptive families are competent but can get overwhelmed when the stressors in their life are out of balance with the resources available to them or when their own skills for solving problems get immobilized because of a pileup of stressors. Focusing on the family's social environment and helping families mobilize their skills to use their network are an important intervention for adoptive families.

In addition, professionals may want to concentrate some of their intervention effort in providing emotional support. Besides providing concrete assistance and information support, it is important to give hope and normalize some of the difficulties that the adopted child and family encounter. Professionals must be available to families to just listen and provide appropriate empathic responses, not being too quick to move to problem solving.

In conclusion, this is only a preliminary study of social support and the adoptive family. Further studies could answer questions about the different use of support groups by parents with children with different categories of special needs. Groups might be most helpful in assisting families parenting children with certain types of problems or issues or at certain developmental points in the adoptive family life cycle.

For instance, although there are concerns common to all adoptive families, support for parents of children with behavioral problems may be different from that needed by parents of children with physical handicaps. Increasing the numbers of groups and participation in them would provide data to further understand the conditions under which they are optimally effective. In addition, there may be different issues in social support for families living in rural areas compared to families living in urban areas. Sampling size did not allow other subgroup analyses such as the differences between white families and families of color and differences between transracial and interracial adoptions. Further studies probing these differences may also be helpful.

7

Integration of Findings with Conceptual Model and Implications

SUMMARY OF FINDINGS

This book reports on a longitudinal study of families who adopted a child or children with special needs. In 1990 a systematic sample was drawn from a list of subsidized adoptions provided by the Iowa Department of Human Services. The information presented in the book is a summary of the responses of 71 families who participated in the 4-year study, which ended in 1993. The sample was biased toward younger children but representative of subsidized adoptions in Iowa on the basis of race and gender. Families who dropped out of the project were not significantly different from families who remained with the project all 4 years. The following summary of findings is put in the context of the resource and stressor model outlined in Chapter 1.

The Community

Most of the stressors and resources outlined in the conceptual model regarding the community were not addressed in this study. Nevertheless, anecdotal information and impressions from the interviews as well as social network data provide insight into the community context of the lives of families. If the social network information provided by these adoptive families is aggregated, most of the social network comprises the community (56%). This includes individuals from clubs, organizations, church, work, school, other friends, and neighbors. In addition, many families had social contact with other adoptive families. Most families reported seeing other adoptive families socially every 2 to 3 months. The vast majority of families report this contact as very or somewhat helpful. Another informal support, a support group

Portions of the material on changing the community and service system were created by Kathy Franz and adapted from a final report (1993) developed for the Adoption Opportunities Grant, "The Post Adoption Family Support Project," located at Northeast Ohio Adoption Services.

for adoptive parents, was not used very often, although those who did attend found it very helpful. However, a significant proportion of families identified support groups for adopted children and adoptive parents as a needed service. Families perceive a great deal of support for the adoption from families and friends, and this support remained consistently high over time. Thus, for the most part, the community and informal supports in the community were positive for these families. Positive community support was a resource that remained steady over the 4 years of the study.

From the anecdotes and interviews with the family, many of the adoptive parents were able to overcome role ambiguity even without community guidelines. There continued to be some anxiety about the adoptive parent role, particularly as the putative rights of the biological father began to get a great deal of national publicity. Some families expressed fear that some member of the biological family of the child could claim their adopted child and have him or her removed from their home, but this was the exception with most of the families. Families had created a niche for themselves in the community as an adoptive family, and most families had gotten confident in their roles over time. Some families became involved in adoption-related activities, both to educate the public about adoption and to normalize adoptive family life in the community.

Overall, from the little evidence gathered from the project, families experience the community as positive. Families had developed informal networks to support the adoption, and most had successfully negotiated role ambiguity.

The Service System

Adoption services were evaluated positively. However, for over one-third of the families, lack of background information on the child was a stressor. One family's story was very compelling in describing the need for complete background information:

The last 2 years have been changing rapidly as far as finding out . . . about my adopted children's past. [Problems] might have been avoided if we had the papers on placements and family history. We are now receiving information, but it didn't help as it would have if we would have been informed of these facts at the beginning. It really wouldn't have changed our minds about adoption . . . . This information is really vital to us as parents. We may be able to avoid problems by knowing in advance what might happen later.

This is our second adoption and with the first we were told all about the background and we read *all* the files on him, so when he came to us with a nightmare or a problem we were able to explain or help him with it. He is doing fairly good and still working through some feelings. But the second adoption . . . we are against a brick wall. We don't understand most of the problems and are looking for help all the time.

So, the bottom line is that these files are very important and should be given to the adopting parents. If they can't handle it at the time they read it, they will never be able to help the child they plan to adopt. . . . By knowing what the child went through before you get them, you could evaluate what problems you will deal with when that child gets older, and you can look into what kind of help may be needed to help that child get through their problems. (adoptive mother, 1992)

This written comment highlights the importance of background information to families. When families did receive information, overall they reported the information was accurate. The biggest problem for a significant proportion of families was getting complete and accurate information.

While preadoptive training experiences were not directly assessed, parents provided written comments about the importance of training. As one mother commented in 1992:

I really think adoptive parents should be required to have more training on adopting older special needs children that would include hearing other parents that did it say "it's not like the Brady Bunch." I was under the mistaken idea that you could adopt a child, give it lots of love and it would make everything all right for them. That is not always true. Some things you can never make right for them. It's also not a guarantee that if you love them that they will love and trust you and bond to you because sometimes that doesn't happen.

The vast majority of families, because they adopted through the public agency, had participated in some type of training. The quality of training and types of training that are most helpful in preparing families for adoption are not known. The type of training that most effectively prepares families for adoption needs further research and development.

Over time there is an increase in participation in both individual and family therapy. Families generally evaluate therapy services positively. Most families report that therapy services are helpful, and their evaluation of services remained fairly consistent over the 4 years of the study.

In evaluating gaps in services, families identified financial support, routine medical and dental care, case management, counseling around adoption issues, and educational services as unmet needs. These gaps in services were a stressor for some families.

Overall, the components of the service system were positive for most families. Suggestions that the service system was a resource for most families are consistent with expectations, given that these were intact families. When the different components of the service system were stressors, there was evidence that they negatively affected the adoption.

The Family System

The adoptive placements were very stable during the 4 years, with very few children spending time in out-of-home placements. As stated before, families had a great deal of support for the adoption, and this support remained consistent. Family functioning changed over the 4 years, with families decreasing their adaptability and cohesion. However, families were still more flexible and close than would be expected of biological families at the same point in their life cycle.

If children's attachment patterns and behaviors change, for the most part, they become more problematic. While not assessed directly, extrapolating from the interviews with parents, parents who were able to change their expectations seem to be the most successful. If parents are going to be able to maintain these children in the home, they must be willing and able to change what they can tolerate in parent/child relations and the behaviors the children will demonstrate. As 1 mother reported in 1990:

We expected kids would have many adjustment problems based on what we were told by social workers. That was a laugh. They had each other [sibling group placement] and [my husband] and I had the adjustment problems! Each problem that came up was an absolute major crisis and it took us three or four years to realize that you just go from day to day. Developing perspective was the hardest part.

Two years later the same mother reports:

We were told many things about how the children would react to the adoption. . . . What no one told us was that the people having the most problems would be us! Probably the hardest thing to learn was that today's problem may be of no consequence tomorrow and that chances are, no one decision will be a life or death one--perspective comes with experience and time. Then when you can relax and go with the flow, the better off you'll be. I don't know that this can be taught at all, but some ought to try. The focus of adoption preparation is on the child(ren); some attention should be paid to the way anyone reacts to a major life change.

For parents who were either unprepared for what to expect or unable to change their expectation to match the capacity of the child, outcomes over time were distinctly more negative. As 1 parent reported:

Overall our home life has deteriorated and now . . . his . . . brother is . . . having problems. Our concerns are doubled and after six years of trying to cope we are wearing thin. We ask ourselves how we ever got into this situation and how will we last about seven or eight years. (adoptive mother, 1992)

Even with continued behavior difficulties and a trend to less positive parent/child relations, outcomes continue to be positive overall. There were many victories for these adoptive parents, and the parents who could focus on the little positive changes that occur evaluated the experiences more favorably. One mother who adopted a boy with physical disabilities commented about his progress in regular school and his move to independent living in a small group home so he could be an independent adult. Another mother commented (1990):

What has been most rewarding about this child's adoption is watching and feeling the bond grow between us. Watching her change from a 3 year old with no speech to a 5 year old with very adequate communication skills. And especially watching her learn that hugs and kisses are fun. I still remember the first time she returned a hug and said "I love you Mom."

Another wrote in 1993:

When I first filled out this questionnaire my child was severely disabled--not able to communicate--age 3.5 but verbal skills at 24 months. Now he is too "verbal" at school. [I'm] amazed at the progress made when I step back and look at the overall picture.

Still another mother commented in 1990:

Alicia is a strong-willed little survivor who has brought much joy to this family and taught me much not only about parenting but about surviving some pretty difficult life situations. She's a *great* kid--just being her parent is rewarding!

The next year the mother reported:

Alicia is a part of our family as much as any biological child could ever be, so *everything* about the adoption is rewarding including the usual ups and downs of parenting! [She] is a warm, loving and kind little girl.

Flexibility in expectations, flexibility in family functioning, and positive, consistent support for the adoption were resources for most families.

The Child as a Subsystem

The educational experiences of the children were generally positive and a resource to the families. Sibling placements have a modest negative effect on parent/child relations and the issues faced by the families. Both adopting a sibling group and adopting children separated from siblings had unique stressors for families. Many children demonstrated significant behavior difficulties, and these difficulties were more pronounced for children with a preadoptive history of physical and sexual abuse. Thus, child behavior was a continual stressor in the adoptive families.

Parent/child relations became more negative over time, although the majority of parents continue to feel quite positive about their children. Problems with attachment and parent/child relations were most apparent for children with a preadoptive history of physical and sexual abuse.

Overall, attachment difficulties and accompanying behavior problems were a significant stressor in families. In addition, families parenting a child who had a preadoptive history of maltreatment had more stressors from behavior problems and attachment difficulties. Attachment difficulties and behavior problems are associated with less favorable adoption outcomes. However, even with the continued difficulties, families remained positive about the adoption.

INCREASING RESOURCES TO ADOPTIVE FAMILIES

The previous section summarized the results from the data provided by the families. This section discusses the implications of the findings. The implications for community change and changing the service system are offered in the context of 2 models. One approach focuses on competence, and the other focuses on system development.

Adler (1982) discusses the competence of communities and the ecological interaction among individuals, families, and communities. Community competence refers to the notion that the community has the resources or means to achieve meeting the needs of its members. The emphasis in a competent community model is building the linkages among the community, the family and the individual. For example, an individual's competence is strengthened if he/she gains skills in interacting with others. A family struggling to have their needs met in the environment in which they live might become more competent through teaching that enhances the family's ability to interact with the environment. The notion that the community is competent and attempts to bring individuals, families, and communities together is part of larger reform movements currently going on in the United States. The often quoted African proverb "It takes a community to raise a child" seems to be a slogan driving the movement to focusing on the community and building on strengths in the community.

In addition to Adler's emphasis on competence, Maquire (1991) offers system development as a way to think about the community and postadoption services. System development is a coordinated effort to combine both formal and informal helpers into a unified system centered on a client/family. Maquire sees this as different from case management that involves only the formal service system. While he focuses on system development for an individual client, it seems possible to expand the concept to the community level. The community needs assistance to develop into a community that is family-centered and supports the diverse families found in the community.

Community Change

Advocacy through public education is part of community change. As part of adoption advocacy, there is a critical need for public education campaigns that present accurate information about adoption, adoptive parents, adoptees, and birth parents. This must include working with the media to provide this information. It also means working with the media and other information sources to use language that is sensitive to adoption.

Community change is also accomplished by establishing community support for adoptive families. Part of garnering community support for adoption is to work with the formal and informal information systems in the community. It might include outreach through local libraries in an effort to purchase and feature books about adoption for children and parents. It also means helping people in the community see an adoptive family as a family that they will support and help in times of difficulties. The parent/child bond in adoptive families needs to be viewed as being just as valued, valid, and worthy of preserving as the parent/child bond in families related by birth. In essence, adopted children belong to the community as much as do children born to parents.

Community change also encompasses increasing and educating the system of informal support. Examples of enhancing families' networks of informal supports might include developing "buddy families." This means developing families who can link with adoptive parents in an informal arrangement. Efforts to educate informal social support networks about adoption could include providing grandparents, aunts or uncles, other extended family members, coworkers, neighbors, and friends with a better understanding of child and family issues in adoption. This, in turn, might increase support from members of the extended, informal community.

System development is concerned with the interface between the family system and the community in which they live. System development includes educating service providers about the needs of the client population, advocating for and with the client population for modifying existing services, and developing programs if the community does not have the services needed by the client population. For adoption this may mean educating the school personnel and mental health providers about adoption. It might mean working with the mental health system to develop day treatment or respite programs for adoptees or working with the existing programs to make them sensitive to the unique issues adopted children and their families bring to these programs. It might mean joining with adoptive parents to advocate with the legislature for postlegal adoption subsidy or working with judges and probation officers to promote better understanding about children with special needs and the families who adopt them. Again, when the informal systems are included, and we move closer to a system development model at the macrolevel, work might include linking self-help groups with one another and developing a "warm line" of adoptive parents willing to listen to other adoptive parents in crisis. It might include the nurturing, founding, and linking of adoptive parent support groups into a coalition of such groups and linking them with other service providers, both formal and informal, who are part of adoptive families' system of helpers. These coalitions can then become a force in the community for promoting change and sensitivity to adoptive families.

Changing the Service System

Child welfare services in general and the adoption service system in particular need reform. The adoption process needs to be more user-friendly, more accessible, and easier to navigate. Home studies need to be a planning document on how to help families prepare to adopt and not a device for screening families out of the adoption process. There needs to be consistent and compassionate follow-up of families and children from recruitment to postlegal support services.

Postlegal services (also referred to as postadoptive services) are services directed to adoptive families after the adoption has become legalized and are intended to be available to families as needed. The specific components of postadoption services vary from agency to agency. Various demonstration projects funded by the Federal Adoption Opportunities Act through the U.S. Department of Health and Human Services Children's Bureau have conceptualized these services to include psychotherapeutic services to families, crisis intervention, case management, adoption-related training for mental health professionals and school personnel, adoptive parent support groups, groups for adopted teens, and "concrete" supportive services to families such as subsidy, respite, buddy families, transportation, and medical services. These demonstration projects and various research studies suggest that adoptive families need an array or continuum of services from which they can choose (Rosenthal & Groze, 1992; Groze & Gruenewald, 1991). Not only do different families have different needs, but the needs of any particular family may change over time (Rosenberg, 1992). As part of meeting the needs of individual families, effective solutions need to look also to families' strengths and realize that they have many good solutions to their own problems.

Several issues, then, must be addressed to make changes in the entire service system, including developing resources and strengthening available resources to provide the array of services needed. In addition, there is often a need for case management to help link adoptive families with existing services. Often, in the process of case management, more is learned about gaps in services and areas in need of development to make the continuum of services more complete.

Case management is a term that is bandied around a great deal in the field of social work without a great deal of consensus about how it is defined. Walsh (1991) found in his survey of adoptive families with children with special needs that, by far, the biggest problems with services are, "I don't know what services are available to me and I don't know where the right services are located" (p. 10). This seems to be a call for traditionally defined case management services, linking families with formal service providers. Rothman (1991) makes the point that while case management includes what was traditionally referred as information and referral services and linkage with formal service providers, case management is more. It also includes linkage with informal service providers as well as outreach to the community to educate and enhance linkages and advocacy. This parallels Maquire's (1991) idea of system development. Rothman makes the point that the need for case management services may be long-term, with the intensity of the case managers' activity rising and falling with the family's level of crisis. For some families who have adopted children with special needs, this way of conceptualizing case management seems particularly accurate.

There is also a need for case management to be family-based or family-centered. This approach gives the parents control over which problems are important to address and allows the case manager to work as a partner with the adoptive parents. Supporting the family and the parents without having to identify one family member as "client" and putting the "parent in charge" of services allow postadoption service to validate the parents, give the parents a sense of entitlement, normalize the struggles adoptive families are experiencing, and build on the strengths they have.

In addition to having family-based case management, family members can serve as case managers for their own children. In the absence of formalized postadoption services, this has been happening for years. Many parents possess the case management skills that include knowledge of the formal social service system, arranging services, monitoring services, obtaining financial reimbursements, and advocacy skills; these families are a valuable resource. Adoptive parents with these skills can help other adoptive parents develop these skills and can train service providers to be more responsive to adoptive families. This requires that the postadoption case manager take on a partnership role with the adoptive family as they jointly accomplish case management around a particular child. The relationship between social worker and adoptive parents is more of an alliance than a client/worker relationship.

In providing services, it often becomes apparent that most of the adoptive families who are trying to parent a seriously emotionally or behaviorally disturbed child are involved with a number of service providers, most of whom look upon the child as the client. Families need a linkage with other adoptive parents who have survived such crises and advocacy as they encounter the other systems, which are often not knowledgeable about adoption. For these families in crisis, a case manager can serve as an ally with the parents while offering the parents hope and a way that the child might remain in the home through respite, day treatment, or any creative combination of formal and informal services.

An additional method of service system change and increasing resources to adoptive families is to provide them with comprehensive and complete information about the child or children whom they are adopting. Case workers, adoption workers, and administrators must work diligently to make sure that information is consistently gathered and documented in the files of children in the child welfare system. This recommendation is not easy to implement. Caseloads are too large to keep up on record keeping, and casework positions have been declassified so many caseworkers do not have a background in social work but are required to collect sensitive and comprehensive information.

Working with the Adoptive Family System

Assessment. The life book, ecomap, social network map, life map, and placement genogram (Aust, 1981; Wheeler, 1978; Pinderhughes & Rosenberg, 1990; Young, Corcran-Rumppe, & Groze, 1992; McMillen & Groze, 1994) are particularly helpful tools for assessment and intervention with adoptive families. These tools are discussed in more detail later. In addition, new resource materials examine the unique issues in the adoptive family life cycle (Rosenberg, 1992) as well as practice techniques specifically adapted for the adoptive family (Reitz & Watson, 1992). Understanding and using these tools as well as familiarizing oneself with the growing body of literature about adoptive families can help practitioners work more skillfully and sensitively with adoptive families.

Skill Building. One of the tasks that families must accomplish is to integrate into their family system a child or children who are cautious of closeness and may not have particularly good skills in family living. Flexible families who can deal with children with serious emotional and behavior difficulties as well as the difficulty that children have with intimacy and family life will be more successful than rigid families in this endeavor. Families may need assistance in learning to be adaptable. This can start during adoption preparation. As part of the home study process, families should be assessed in their level of adaptability. When families are less adaptable, this should be seen as an at-risk family. They should not be screened out of the adoption process. Rather, they may need special assistance as part of their preparation for adoption and ongoing support throughout the adoption to enhance their adaptability. After placement, preventive models such as the family-bonding model (Pinderhughes & Rosenberg, 1990) offer a psychoeducational approach to assist with the issues the new adoptive family must resolve.

Families also may need assistance in learning how to remain close to their children even when they behave in provocative, ambivalent and distancing manners; these behaviors need to be reframed as attachment issues. They may need help in learning to separate the behavior from the children as well as to look for opportunities to build attachment with their children. Helping parents gain the skills they need to manage children with behavior difficulties and assisting them in building attachment promote successful adoptions. This might include helping families change the expectations of their children and the type of attachment relationship they can expect to have with their children.

Support System Intervention. Families can be assisted by increasing their resources. In the assessment of resources and stressors to the family, an ecomap (Hartman & Laird, 1983) and social network map (Tracy & Whittaker, 1990) can be helpful. The ecomap visually diagrams the resources and stressors in the life space of the family, and the social network map examines both the structure and function of social networks (see Chapter 6). Both could be used as a way to assess family resources, gaps, and stressors. In addition, by conceptualizing the family as a system of resources and stressors that affect the functioning of the family system, practitioners pave the way for families to use problem-solving skills that may have been underutilized if the problem was defined as child or family dysfunction. This could include the use of services such as respite care to avoid a "pileup" of stressors.

As part of the process of intervention, a practitioner can reaffirm for families that each experience that they successfully resolve increases the likelihood of being successful with other crises. In addition, practitioners can predict for families that they will have crises and help the family plan for dealing with them. The process of planning to deal with a crisis can include helping the family explore what resources are available that they currently use and possible resources that they can turn to that have not been used in the past. When a family begins to envision a future with a mixture of hope and realism, the family can then focus their efforts on how they will go about using the resources, past and present.

Intervention that might increase the family's competence could include giving them knowledge of the stages of identity development in the adoptee and awareness about life cycle issues that affect a family's development. This would increase the family's ability to navigate developmental transitions (Adler, 1982). Interventions to increase competence could also include classes that teach adoptive parenting skills, training in how to be an effective advocate with the schools or other systems, and behavior management techniques for an older and special needs child.

Working with the Child Subsystem

Attachment interventions. Patterns of attachment can be modified. Tizard (1977) suggests that behaviors that are not reinforced lose their effectiveness over time. As children experience caregiving that is positive and consistent over time, their cognitive models of others and themselves are challenged. A significant number of families need some assistance in helping the child overcome their history and helping the family function in a way that decreases the child's negative patterns of attachment. Bowlby (1988) suggests 5 tasks in therapeutic work with persons with attachment difficulties. His recommendations rely on the use of relationship-based cognitive therapy to restructure the client's representation of work, others, self, and relationship to others (see pp. 138-139).

Two instruments that can help both parents and therapist in their cognitive work with children are the life book and the placement genogram. The life book (Wheeler, 1978; Aust, 1981) is a scrapbook that contains photos as well as other mementos, drawings, and memories that form the child's life experiences. It is used to help children connect and integrate their past to the present and assist in planning for the future. If children do not have a life book when they enter adoptive placement, they can be assisted in developing one postplacement that can serve as a guide for addressing past relationship issues.

A second instrument, the placement genogram (Groze, Young, & Corcran-Rumppe, 1991; McMillen & Groze, 1994), is a diagraming technique that traces the child's placement history starting from birth and records pertinent information about each placement. For instance, the date of parental rights termination, allegations of abuse, and relationships with significant caretakers might be documented on the placement genogram. This information can help provide insight into the issues raised by adoptive families as they try to understand the child's behavior and its impact on their family (Hartman & Laird, 1983). The placement genogram also helps the child to explore the meaning of relationships and how those relationships have influenced his or her life. A therapist who helps children unfold their life history can begin to explore the "working models" children have of relationships and help children cognitively restructure the models to increase attachment in the adoptive home. Melina (1986) suggests that adoptive parents can facilitate attachment cognitively by also assisting children in examining and understanding their past, giving children a vision for the future, and using appropriate and positive physical contact.

However, behavioral approaches also must be employed to assist children who have attachment difficulties. Parents should model and express feelings; modeling and expressing feelings are essential components to facilitating attachment between parent and child. In addition, parents need to provide discipline without resorting to emotionally laden words. They need to use natural and logical consequences for transgressions.

Working with Sibling Groups

Preparation of Siblings for Family Placement Together. The complexities of the histories of children and life in the child welfare system create confusion for children. As discussed before, life books, time lines, life maps, and placement genograms assist children (and families) in reducing this confusion. The life book and placement genogram have been discussed. The life map is a picture the child draws that represents his or her life. A curving road is drawn on a poster board, and at the top of the page where the road begins is the child's birth. At the bottom of the page where the road ends is the current living situation of the child. Working with a therapist, the child then diagrams the different places and events of his or her life, including the different homes and any major events that stand out. The time line is a different way to organize the same information. The timeline is graph paper that is taped end-to-end. Each square on the graph represents a month in the life of the child and each placement is color-coded a different color. The timeline provides a visual, color picture of where children have been, and each month they stay in their adoptive home, another square is colored in.

These tools can be used to help siblings understand each other's perceptions and experiences about their history, together and apart, including their history with the birth family. Each sibling can develop his or her own life map and timeline. These maps and timelines can be used to help children piece together their life history and can be shared with each other as part of preadoptive placement preparation. Understanding their experiences and the experiences of their siblings can be beneficial in promoting stability in the adoption and beginning to work together on the unique issues the children bring to the adoptive family system.

Many siblings also need information and practice about "normal" sibling interactions. These issues should be addressed in both individual and sibling therapy sessions. Siblings and prospective families should be aware that individual, sibling, or group therapy may be helpful periodically throughout the children's development. It is important to keep in mind also that these activities are not discrete events but that children may have to go over these many times; each time the children gain a different perspective on the issues involved in their lives.

Preparation of Families for a Sibling Placement. Using a placement genogram that documents significant facts such as abuse history, placement history, or mental health services provides a visual picture of the child and his or her history to the prospective foster and adoptive parents. Knowing this history can be helpful to families. Siblings are likely to re-create or promote family patterns in their foster or adoptive homes that replicate their experiences in the birth family. Prospective families need to be educated about what the dynamics were in previous placements, and family therapy should be included in pre- and postplacement services. Family therapy can assist families in recognizing the problematic interactions and behaviors patterns and empower them to intervene more quickly and effectively to interrupt negative cycles. Families often benefit from developing their own life book that they can share with the children. Part of preparation of children and families for placement should include sharing the life books. In addition, families need additional training to assist them in preparing for the placement of more than one child.

Postplacement Intervention in Families with Siblings. Children define themselves by comparing themselves to significant others; siblings play a critical role in this definition throughout the life span (Pfouts, 1976). Working with the children as a subsystem can help them as they explore their relationship to each other as well as their relationship in the context of the family system in which they were adopted (Hegar, 1988; Ranieri & Pratt, 1978). Intervention for children must include assisting them in finding new roles in the adoptive family system in which they can gain family recognition and self-esteem (see also Pfouts, 1976).

Particular attention needs to be given to attachment between siblings. Individual case studies have shown that children grow more attached to their siblings when they have experienced severe parental losses and neglect or abuse. Their attachment is greater than shown by siblings who have not experienced such losses (Lamb & Sutton-Smith, 1982). Hegar (1988) suggests that biological siblings are better able to help each other than unrelated children and that promoting attachment means preserving the sibling bond (Hegar, 1993). Children placed together offer the continuance of part of the children's own family life, which seems important in adjusting to a new home. This issue has relevance for both foster care and adoption but is even more critical when adoption is a permanent placement compared to foster care, which is supposedly a temporary placement. Thus, postplacement services must include sibling therapy as the children and families work out their new and evolving relationship.

Decision Making on Keeping Siblings Together or Splitting Them Up. The norm should be that siblings are kept together, and only when there is compelling evidence or when interventions into sibling relations fail should consideration be given to separation. There is no doubt that practitioners need to assess high-risk behaviors such as sexual reactivity, sexual offending, and aggression when placing any child in a family. However, these behaviors are not necessary and sufficient evidence to separate siblings. When siblings exhibit or have exhibited aggressive or sexually reactive behaviors with each other, a practitioner must first assess the context of this behavior; that is, the practitioner must have a good understanding of the dynamics of the situation(s) in which this behavior occurs. Second, there needs to be an assessment as to whether any intervention has been given to try to change these behaviors and the effects of any treatment. This information can assist the practitioner in predicting the likelihood of these behaviors' recurring in the prospective family and what treatment interventions may be effective. If the risk of these behaviors' continuing is great, the children's response to treatment has been minimal, and a family cannot be found that will tolerate extreme behaviors, placing siblings apart can be considered. Once the decision is made, the practitioner and prospective families should explore how to maintain sibling ties, although the children will be in separate locations. In addition, effort must be given to assisting the siblings with loss and grief issues as they separate from each other.

Preparation of Siblings for Family Placement Apart. Whether children are placed together or apart, the same tools and issues pertinent to siblings placed together apply to siblings placed apart. At a minimum, in a day and age of high-tech copy machines, there is every reason to duplicate all parts of individual life books. In fact, as Kupecky (1993) points out, it is best to photocopy all components, pictures, and so on. and place the original in a file. Then, when parts of the book get lost or destroyed, copies of the originals can be made again.

Additional issues for siblings placed apart are the loss of the sibling relationship and gaining an understanding of what the sibling relationship will "look like" in the future. Siblings who are living together prior to being placed apart experience loss and grief related to the separation, regardless of the quality of the relationship. Siblings need to know why they are being separated, have an opportunity to recognize the change through rituals such as letters, cards, or videotapes, and have a clear understanding of what the sibling interactions will be in the future. Siblings who are already placed separately need to understand why they will continue to be separated and what their ongoing contact will be with their sibling(s). It is helpful for siblings to have an opportunity to meet the other's parent(s) and know when their next contact will be and how it will occur. It is incumbent upon the adults to take the initiative to plan and facilitate ongoing contact.

8

The Future of Adoption

The nature of what has traditionally been defined as a special need in adoption is changing. In the 1970s, a special need was defined as being older at placement (usually school age), having a physical, emotional, or behavior handicap, membership in a sibling group, a history of abuse, minority group status, or some combination of these needs. While these descriptions are still relevant, the term *special need* has had to be expanded. The 1980s introduced a new wave of medically fragile children to child welfare; many children were entering child welfare affected by crack cocaine and other drugs as well as children infected with HIV. At the same time, the fall of communism in the 1990s and the expansion of the United States into a global economy has increased contact with other countries and the adoption of children from Eastern Europe and other formerly communist countries. These children have unique health and developmental problems; many of the adopted children were older and had experienced extreme poverty and neglect. Children affected by HIV, substance abuse, or international adoption represent new challenges in adoption services, policy, and practice.

MEDICALLY FRAGILE CHILDREN

Drug Affected Children

Estimates of the number of infants born with exposure to illegal drugs each year range from 30,000 (Besharov, 1989) to 375,000 (Schneider, Griffith & Chasnoff, 1989), with 150,000 probably being the best estimate (Gomly & Shiono, 1991). Due to inconsistent screening and testing within the health care system, accurate counts of the total problem are unavailable. Estimates of the number of drug-affected children entering or at risk of entering the child welfare system are also problematic. Though only a modest proportion of drug-exposed children enter the child welfare system at birth, many may later enter the child welfare system due to the chaotic and dangerous home environment of drug-abusing parents. In one study (General Accounting Office

[GAO], 1990) an estimated 30% of children born drug-affected in 1989 were placed in foster care at birth. Officials in New York State estimate that 75% of foster care children come from alcohol- and other drug-abusing families (Child Welfare League of America [CWLA], 1990). Nationally, it is estimated that 30% to 50% of drug exposed children enter foster care (FOCUS, 1990).

The difficulties encountered by drug-exposed children are not uniform (Zuckerman, 1993). The short-term and long-term effects of drug exposure on the child vary with the type of drug used, frequency of usage by the mother, the length of time the drug is used, and when drug usage occurs in the pregnancy. Some drug-exposed infants may suffer significant medical problems. They may have delays in psychomotor development (Chasnoff et al., 1986; Little et al., 1989), difficulties in temperament, sleep, or attachment behavior (Wachsman et al., 1989), and problems in physical development (Smith et al., 1986; Kaye et al., 1989). Long-term studies indicate that some drug-exposed children exhibit poor motor skills, speech and language delays, short attention span, extreme apathy or aggressiveness, and difficulty in forming attachments with others (Cohen, Dinsmore, & Repella, 1989). The difficulties generated by prenatal drug exposure may require regular medical and neurobehavioral evaluations and early interventions to meet the needs of the developing child as well as early intervention to assist families who are dealing with children who may have a lag or difficulties in development.

However, these results do not necessarily present an accurate understanding of the effects of drug exposure. The lack of longitudinal information about outcomes for drug-exposed children and the horror stories about the difficulties of caring for drug-exposed children may have been exaggerated. Although the GAO (1990) early findings on drug-exposed children raised concerns over the ability of parents to meet long-term needs of these children, evidence is mounting that adopting drug-exposed children is not substantially different from adopting other children (Barth, 1991; Barth & Needell, in press).

That is not to say that drug exposure has no effects on children but to highlight that the difficulties are not profound for the majority of children. In addition, it is important to recognize the obstacles faced in promoting the adoption of children born affected by drugs. One of the greatest obstacles is the lack of information about what the future holds for children born affected by drugs.

Children with HIV or AIDS

The first acknowledged case of pediatric acquired immunodeficiency syndrome (AIDS) occurred in 1982. This event marked a rapid progression in the identification of this childhood illness. Through 1993 the Centers for Disease Control (CDC) reported over 4,000 cases of pediatric AIDS for children less than 13 years of age; this represents about 2% of the AIDS population (CDC, 1992). For every child with AIDS, 3 to 5 children are infected with the HIV virus (Novick, 1989; Oleske, 1987). Given 1993 reports from the CDC, this would suggest that over 12,000 to over 20,000 children are infected with HIV. Gwinn, Pappaioanou and George (1991) estimate that up to 80,000 women of childbearing age may currently be infected with HIV. This means that 1,500 to 2,100 babies could be born with HIV in the United States each year. Most cases (85%) of pediatric AIDS were transmitted from mother to child; 13% resulted from exposure through transfusions or products associated with a hemophilia/coagulation disorder, and 2% were undetermined (CDC, 1992).

Pediatric AIDS cases are overrepresented among ethnic and racial minority groups. In the United States, white children represent 75% of the child population and only 21% of pediatric AIDS cases; Hispanic children represent 10% of the child population and 25% of AIDS cases; black children represent 15% of the child population but 53% of pediatric AIDS cases (Quinn, 1987; Hutchings, 1988; Select Committee, 1988; CDC, 1992).

Children with HIV or AIDS have many health issues. One study observed that the birth height and weight of HIV-infected children ranked in the 15th and 24th percentiles, respectively (Leeds, 1992); this places children at increased risk for developmental disabilities. Head circumference, a measurement often associated with intelligence, falls below the average with HIV- infected children, scoring at the 20th percentile. Several studies found the majority of children with HIV have neurological and developmental abnormalities (Rubinstein, 1989; Johnson et al., 1989). By 1995, it is estimated that HIV may become the largest infectious cause of mental retardation and encephalopathy in children under the age of 13 (Crocker, Cohen, & Kastner, 1992).

The care needed by children with AIDS or HIV can include vigorous nutritional support, early hospitalization for treatment of infections, and monthly prophylactic therapy or treatment (Oleske, 1987; Rubinstein, 1987). The major health problems include failure to thrive and chronic bacterial infections; children also may have chronic pneumonia, developmental delays, and neurological abnormalities. Their medical care and prophylactic treatment require ongoing contact with a multitude of pediatric specialists and multiple service providers.

The growing number of children with HIV or AIDS threatens to strain an already burdened child welfare system. Often, these children enter the child welfare system for another reason, such as parental substance abuse. In one state, before their diagnosis 40% of these children were known to the state's child welfare agency (Boland et al., 1988). Their HIV status is often discovered after foster care placement. A growing number of children are entering the child welfare system once their parent becomes too ill to care for them (Anderson, 1986). One study suggests that 55% to 60% of children with HIV infection are in foster care (Hopkins, 1989), although the most common estimate approximates that 25% to 33% of infants born with AIDS or HIV enter substitute care (Tourse & Gundersen, 1988; Boland et al., 1988).

There is uncertainty about the rate at which children with HIV or AIDS are promoted for adoption (cf., Groze, Haines-Simeon, & Barth, 1994). In one study (Children Awaiting Parents [CAP], 1992) 16 states identified a total of 962 HIV children. Eighty-four (9%) of the infected children were free for adoption. In addition, the study was able to identify 102 children infected with HIV or antibody positive from 12 states having been adopted in the past 3 years (CAP, 1992). Many of these children were being adopted by their foster parents. The results from CAP suggest that adoption may not be promoted as a permanency plan for children infected with HIV or AIDS.

Barriers in Adoption of Medically Fragile Children

One major barrier for parents willing to adopt a child born affected by drugs or with HIV or AIDS is the issue of subsidy rates. Families are fearful that the special funding available to foster and adoptive parents could eventually be cut from state budgets; some foster families elect guardianship or long-term foster care rather than risk the chance of being saddled with huge medical bills by becoming an adoptive family (Markese & Soule, 1992; Emery, Anderson & Annin, 1992). Related to the issue of subsidy is the fear of assuming the burden of financial responsibility for medical care of the child once the adoption has been confirmed (Groze, Haines-Simeon, & Barth, 1994). Since much is unknown, families are reluctant to make a commitment to adoption if they fear that future medical expenses may exceed their resources.

Other barriers include the lack of family, service system, and community support (Groze, Haines-Simeon, & McMillen, 1992; Groze, McMillen, & Haines-Simeon, 1993), particularly for children with HIV or AIDS. Families report that they are not given enough information about the child, and most do not feel that the services that are provided postplacement are helpful. In addition, the private system of medical care created difficulty for some parents in finding routine medical care for their children. Finally, the social arena of fear and uncertainty surrounding the issue of caring for children with HIV or AIDS is a barrier; extended family and friends can be very unsupportive to families caring for a child who has such a disease.

Another source of difficulty is the lack of receptivity to adoption on the part of adoption agencies and the legal system. This is clearest in the length of time it takes to get a case through the court. The length of time to complete the adoption process can take up to several years, proving to be detrimental to a terminally ill child (Emery, Anderson, & Annin, 1992).

Thus, states and agencies are dealing with children who were born drug-affected and/or with HIV or who develop AIDS and need adoptive families. These children represent new challenges to an old system. If there is commitment that all children are adoptable, these new medically fragile children will offer unique challenges in keeping this commitment.

INTERNATIONAL ADOPTION

International adoption has occurred for many years. There has been a steady stream of children from foreign countries entering the United States for adoption over the last decade. Figure 8.1 presents data that estimate the number of adoptions per year over 10 years by major geographic areas. According to these estimates provided by Adoptive Families of America and based on the number of visas issued, over 7,000 children are adopted internationally each year. There has been a steady decrease in the number of children adopted from Asia and, beginning in 1990, an increase in adoptions from Europe. The adoptions from Europe, particularly in 1991, predominantly were from Romania. By 1993 this had changed to children coming from republics of the former Soviet Union.

The fall of communism added new children to the population of children adopted internationally. The opening of adoption in the former communist countries presents some unique problems. This section focuses on the children from Romania because it is the country that involved the majority of European adoptions in the early 1990s. In addition, the issues in Romania have many similarities to the issues from other former communist countries.

In 1990 news programs brought the attention of the world to the difficulties that thousands of children faced living in institutions in Romania. This knowledge brought an immediate response from numerous agencies and individuals from around the

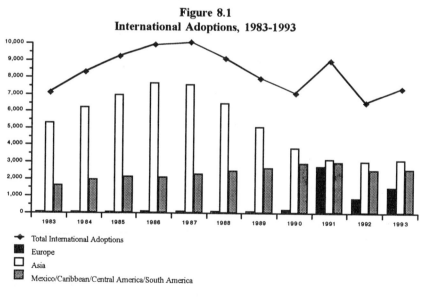

Figure 8.1
International Adoptions, 1983-1993

◆ Total International Adoptions
■ Europe
□ Asia
▨ Mexico/Caribbean/Central America/South America

Source: Adoptive Families of America

world who traveled to Romania to provide supplies, infrastructure repair, personnel, training, technical assistance, and humanitarian aid. The images of suffering so vivid in the media were the consequence of years of poor public policy and denial of social problems.

The problems started in the 1960s with a series of pronatalist policies aimed at increasing the population of the country. These policies included rigorous anticontraceptive propaganda campaigns, restricted access to legal abortions, and taxation of childless couples (Roberts, 1984; Haupt, 1987). While large families were encouraged, there were virtually no government assistance to strengthen or support families, little public health information about prenatal care, and restricted diets.

When it became apparent that some children could not be cared for in their family, a system of institutions was developed. The institutions that served as the entrance into the child welfare system were labeled orphanages. Children were placed here until the age of 3. At age 3, an assessment was conducted, usually by a physician. There were no uniformity in the assessment process and little evidence of the training of the many people who were making placement decisions. Children were evaluated as normal, handicapped, or "irrecoverable." Children who were evaluated as "normal" were sent to training schools. Children who showed some delay or minor physical difficulty were sent to schools for the handicapped. Children whose problems were judged to be too severe for either of these placements were sent to institutions for the "irrecoverable." This included children with major mental and physical disabilities as well as children with medically correctable handicaps such as cross-eyes or club feet. Gypsy children were disproportionately labeled irrecoverable.

There were many problems with all the institutions (cf. Johnson & Groze, 1993). The conditions of the buildings were initially adequate but over time became in disrepair. Information from the noncommunist countries (i.e., "the West") became increasingly restricted so that all the child development and developmental disability research was denied to doctors, nursing assistants, and staff at the many institutions. The nursing assistants (child care workers) were required to care for too many children. For example, it was not unusual for women to be assigned from 8 to 35 children, all of whom could be bedridden or unable to feed themselves. Even with healthy toddlers and children, a median ratio of 10 to 1 was impractical because it restricts personal interactions and provides limited opportunities for reinforcement or praise (McMullan & Fisher, 1992; McMullan, Ames, & Chisholm, submitted). Finally, there were scant records or documentation on these children, and records did not follow children from institution to institution. At the same time, children were transferred from one location to another, often without notice to the family (Johnson & Groze, 1993). The result was substandard institutions, grossly inadequate child care and thousands of children being raised without a family. The institutions for the irrecoverable had the worst conditions and the highest child mortality.

By the end of the Ceausescu regime it was estimated that there were over 600 institutions housing 100,000 to 200,000 children (Ceccherini, 1991; Hines, Kessler & Landers, 1991). A significant number of children were infected with HIV. Most of the children had been infected from blood transfusions, which were routine procedures in some locations to help low-birth-weight babies get a "boost" in their development. This policy of transfusing dystrophic babies resulted in over half the children with HIV in Europe being located in Romania.

After the "revolution" in December 1989, Romania became a more open country. Visa restrictions were lifted, and foreigners were encouraged, or at least not actively discouraged, to visit Romania. It was no longer forbidden to speak with foreigners, and a trickle of nationals from European and American countries began to enter the country. As media reports brought the world's attention to the thousands of abandoned children residing in institutions, independent adoptions quickly became the norm. Initially, persons wishing to adopt could privately go to an orphanage and view a child or several children, depending on the individual policy and practice of the orphanage, and choose a child to adopt. A fee was usually paid to the administrator, although some administrators recognized that families were better than orphanages and refused to accept fees. For a nominal fee, an attorney could be hired to process the adoption in Romania. The process usually included securing a parent's signature for relinquishment, approving the family as adoptive parents in Romania, obtaining a passport for the child from the Romanian government, and obtaining an emigration visa for the child from the American Embassy.

At first, this was an easy process that cost very little (approximately $2000). However, as the demand for these children increased, and the people involved in the process (lawyers, administrators, birth parents, brokers) came to know the potential earnings for helping people seeking to adopt children, the "system" became out of control. Since the average monthly salary in Romania at that time was about $40, costs soon increased so that everyone could benefit fiscally. This included the aforementioned people and, as the legal system began to process more applications, the judges and finally the politicos who had a part in issuing passports. Soon many families became discouraged with the bureaucracy and traveling from orphanage to orphanage. They then turned to baby-broker intermediaries to locate and arrange the financial and legal transactions to obtain babies and toddlers.

As the process of adoption became open, and more families traveled to Romania, there was also a movement away from adopting children living in the institution to securing the adoption of children living in families, many of which were poor and single-parent families. Children most in need of being adopted, that is, the institutionalized children, were seen as second-choice.

This system led to the exploitation and exportation of Romania's children and resulted in worldwide criticism. In June 1991 a moratorium was placed on adoptions, and legislation was drafted to deal with the problems generated by the black market. As of 1991 all adoptions are processed through the Romanian Committee on Adoption and licensed international adoption agencies (Johnson, Edwards, & Puwak, 1993).

The result is that many children were adopted from institutional settings as well as from black market transactions. Little is known about how these children and families are faring. There is some reason to be concerned. Many of these families, at least initially, seemed to ignore or minimize the potential effects of preadoptive history on the adjustment and development of the child. There have been anecdotal reports of families abandoning these children after they were brought to the United States because the children had significant developmental problems. The social and developmental lags in the children reared in institutional settings should not have been a surprise, given previous research on the effects of institutionalization on children (Bowlby, 1951; Dennis, 1973; Freud & Burlingham, 1973; Provence & Lipton, 1962; Spitz, 1945). Kaler and Freeman (1994) and Cermack (1994), studying children under the age of 5 living in Romanian institutions, found that all the children exhibited deficits in cognitive and social functioning, and the majority were severely delayed. Johnson and colleagues (1992) found that the majority of children had health problems and that the longer the institutionalization, the greater the developmental lag.

While these studies can document the negative effect of institutions on child development, what is not known is the effect living in a family can have on reversing negative effects. Clearly, though, families who are not prepared for dealing with children with disabilities and are not able to modify their expectations of children put the adoptive placement at risk. Much more information is needed as adoption expands to the international arena.

CHALLENGES TO ADOPTION SERVICES, POLICY, AND PRACTICE

Adoption services, policy, and practice are always evolving. Problems arise when the field of adoption and adoption programs, policies, or practices are out of sync. There is a great risk of difficulties arising if current challenges are not effectively resolved. Since there are still federal mandates to promote permanency through adoption for children who cannot remain or be reunified with the extended biological family, several service, policy, and practice issues must be addressed.

Recruitment must be a priority if families are to be found to care for medically fragile children. To effectively recruit, funding is necessary to assist agencies in recruitment activities. Families can be found who are willing to adopt children infected with HIV or affected by substance abuse. It appears that if agencies can be successful in locating foster families, a number of these families may become fost-adopt families (Groze, McMillen, & Haines-Simeon, 1993). These are families who start as foster families and later decide to adopt the children they foster. Strategies should include targeting people who are employed in human service areas such as health, medicine, and social services or people active in religious organizations.

Some families face enormous challenges and strains in adopting medically fragile children. Adoptive families of children with HIV may need help in education planning, case management, or dealing with emotional difficulties for having to contact and arrange services from multiple agencies, as well as dealing with issues of life and death. It is essential to have personnel who will work with the public and private services to coordinate a continuum of services for these families (Boland et al., 1988;

Woodruff & Sterzin, 1988). The same issue also applies to some of the families who adopt internationally. Many of these families were not adequately prepared for the adoption and are unsophisticated in navigating the service system. If their child has difficulties, they may need assistance in securing a range of services to meet the needs of the child and family.

One service routinely not available to adoptive families is respite care. Respite care provides a period of temporary relief or rest from parental responsibilities. Respite care for a family caring for a medically fragile child is essential. Getting a baby-sitter for any child with medical difficulties is troublesome. The availability of respite care would make it easier to care for medically needy children, such as children with HIV or drug exposure, and to recruit foster and adoptive families for them (Tourse & Gundersen, 1988). In one program providing foster care for children with AIDS, the average foster family received approximately 32 hours of relief help weekly (Gurdin & Anderson, 1987). If this is an indication of the support necessary to maintain a medically needy child in a home, then respite care may be an essential service to strengthen and preserve adoptive families.

Many children with HIV and some children born drug-affected have handicaps. Also, many children adopted internationally with histories of prolonged institutionalization, deprivation, and neglect suffer from an array of handicaps or disabilities. Section 504 of the Rehabilitation Act of 1973 can be helpful in planning for the educational needs of these children. Educational systems are mandated to provide for the educational needs of all children. While so mandated, meeting educational needs can be a challenge to both the parents and the school. The children's learning problems or special needs can be quite draining on the school resources. Also, the school may not understand the intricacies of the child's needs. This might require the parents and workers to be strong advocates in the school setting for the children. One way to assist in education programming is to help the school system become more acquainted with HIV issues and concerns, the effects of substance abuse, deprivation, and neglect on children's learning, and information about adoption issues in general. Advocacy and public education then become critical postlegal adoption services.

The development of subsidies has been one of the most beneficial programs to assist families. However, there are a few problems with the subsidy programs. Adoption subsidies are lower than foster care payments and do not increase as the child gets older. Clearly, the lower payment can add financial stress to families who experience stress as they try to integrate a child or children into the family. In addition, most states do not allow families who adopt internationally to participate in state subsidy programs. This policy needs to be reexamined, particularly if the lack of subsidy places the adoption at risk. States would be well advised to be flexible in their subsidy program if a subsidy will help strengthen and preserve a family adopting internationally. Failure to do so will be more costly if the child enters the child welfare system because the family is unable to provide the resources necessary to meet the child's needs.

In addition to subsidy flexibility, in some cases Medicaid benefits are extended to the child after adoption as part of the placement agreement. However, even with Medicaid benefits extended after adoption, there are increasing concerns that state Medicaid programs provide only limited access to the health care services needed by the children in the child welfare system (Schorr, 1987). The provision of subsidy continues to be a good plan, although modification of existing practices and policies is warranted.

Finally, adoption preparation activities need to be tailored to these unique situations. Caring for a medically fragile child or parenting a child who has been institutionalized or severely deprived early in life requires great skill and dedication. Current adoption preparation activities are not sufficient to help families prepare for these challenges. New curriculum needs to be developed, and existing curriculum needs to be modified to meet the needs of families who want to adopt the new wave of special needs children.

CONCLUSION

There will always be new issues to tackle in child welfare and in adoption. Medically fragile children and the stream of international adoptions represent ongoing issues. Research in adoption needs to explore these new issues. In addition, other significant gaps remain. Little is known about the life of older and special needs adoptees as they reach adulthood. These outcomes need to be compared to the outcomes for children who stayed with the birth family, children raised in foster care, and children raised in group or residential care to understand the long-term consequences of these various arrangements. There also needs to be more integrative work that compares and contrasts the experiences of children placed as infants and children placed when older in adoptive families. Much of the research and practice seems to divide adoption into two poles, and much is to be learned from integrating our knowledge in practice, theory, and research.

A major problem with adoption research is the lack of funding. Without consistent, well-funded projects, researchers are forced to piece together small projects that help fill the gaps in knowledge but fall far short of providing some of the answers to adoption questions. Many of the limitations in this study (dropouts, lack of the child's perspective over the 4 years) could have been mitigated if funding for adoption research had been provided. Both the federal government and private foundations could take a more active role in adoption research without limiting the research to problems (e.g., mental health difficulties) or evaluation activities as part of adoption demonstration projects or child welfare reform.

A significant part of the child population is affected by adoption. In addition, many other people are affected by each adoptive placement. Adoption, while it may change, is here to stay, and we need to have better information that is based in research. There are difficulties and unique issues that families and children must face as they navigate a life together. Nevertheless, it is a social arrangement that has more positives than it does negatives and remains the best solution for children who cannot be raised with their biological parents.

References

Aber, J. L., & Allen, J. P. (1987). Effects of Maltreatment on Young Children's Socioemotional Development: An Attachment Theory Perspective. *Developmental Psychology* 23(3):406-414.

Achenbach, T. (1991). *Manual for the Child Behavior Checklist/4-18 and 1991 Profile.* Burlington: University of Vermont, Department of Psychiatry.

Achenbach, T., & Edelbrock, C. (1983). *Manual for the Child Behavior Checklist.* Burlington: University of Vermont, Department of Psychiatry.

Adler, P. (1982). An Analysis of the Concept of Competence in Individuals and Social Systems. *Community Mental Health Journal* 18:35-45.

Ainsworth, M. D. S. (1973). The Development of Infant-Mother Attachment. In B. M. Caldwell & H. N. Ricciutti, ed., *Review of Child Development Research*, Vol. 3. Chicago: University of Chicago Press, 1-94.

Aldridge, M., & Cautley, P. (1975). The Importance of Worker Availability in the Functioning of New Foster Homes. *Child Welfare* Vol. 54(6):444-453.

American Humane Association. (1988). *Highlights of Official Child Abuse and Neglect Reporting-1986.* Denver: Author.

Anderson, G. R. (1986). *Children and AIDS: The Challenge for Child Welfare.* Washington, DC: Child Welfare League of America.

Aust, P. H. (1981). Using the Life Story Book in Treatment of Children in Placement. *Child Welfare* 60(8):535-560.

Bachrach, C. A. (1986). Adoptive Plans, Adopted Children, and Adoptive Mothers. *Journal of Marriage and the Family* 48(2):243-253.

Bachrach, C. A., Adams, P. F., Sambrano, S., & London, K. A. (1989). Advance Data: Adoption in the 1980s. Advance Data from Vital and Health Statistics, Hyattsville, MD: (U.S. Department of Health and Human Services, Public Health Service, CDC & Prevention) National Center for Health Statistics.

Bailey, K. D. (1987). *Methods of Social Research*, 3d ed. New York: Free Press.

Bank, S., & Kahn, M. D. (1982). *The Sibling Bond.* New York: Basic Books.

Barth, R. (1988). Disruption in Older Child Adoptions. *Public Welfare* Winter:323-329.

———. (1991). Adoption of drug-exposed children. *Children and Youth Services Review* 13, 323-342.

Barth, R. P., & Berry, M. (1988). *Adoption and Disruption: Rates, Risks, and Response.* New York: Aldine de Gruyter.

Barth, R. P., Berry, M., Carons, M. L., Goodfield, R., & Feinberg, B. (1986). Contributors to Disruption and Dissolution of Older Child Adoptions. *Child Welfare* 65(4):359-370.

Barth, R. P., Berry, M., Yoshikami, R., Goodfield, R. K., & Carson, M. L. (1988). Predicting Adoption Disruption. *Social Work* 33:227-233.

Barth, R. P., & Needell, B. (in press). Outcomes for Drug-Exposed Children Four Years Post-adoption. *Children and Youth Services Review*.

Bath, H. I., & Haapala, D. A. (1993). Intensive Family Preservation Services with Abused and Neglected Children: An Examination of Group Differences. *Child Abuse and Neglect* 17:213-225.

Beitchman, J. H., Zucker, K. J., Hood, J. E., DaCosta, G. A., Akman, D., & Cassavia, E. (1992). A Review of the Long-Term Effects of Child Sexual Abuse. *Child Abuse and Neglect* 16:101-118.

Belsky, C. J. (1980). Child maltreatment: An Ecological Integration. *American Psychologist* 35(April):320-335.

Berry, M., & Barth, R. P. (1989). Behavior Problems of Children Adopted When Older. *Children and Youth Services Review* 11:221-238.

Besharov, D. (1989). The Children of Crack: Will We Protect Them? *Public Welfare* 47(4):6-11.

Betz, N. E. (1987). Use of Discriminant Analysis in Counseling Psychology Research. *Journal of Counseling Psychology* 34(4):393-403.

Blakeslee, S. (1990). Parents Fear for Future of Infants Born to Drugs. *New York Times*, May 19, pp. 1, 8-9.

Blalock, H. M. (1979). *Social Statistics*, revised 2d ed. St. Louis: McGraw-Hill.

Bohman, M. (1971). A Comparative Study of Adopted Children, Foster Children, and Children in their Biological Environment Born after Undesired Pregnancies. *Acta Pediatrica Scandinavia* (Suppl. 221).

Bohman, M., & Sigvardsson, S. (1980). A Prospective Longitudinal Study of Children Registered for Adoptions: A 15-Year Follow-Up. *Acta. Psychiatrica Scandinavia* 61:90-97.

_____. (1982). Adoption and Fostering as Preventive Measures. In E. J. Anthony & C. Chiland, eds., *The Child in His Family*. New York: Wiley, 171-180.

Boland, M. G., Allen, T. J., Long, G. I., & Tasker, M. (1988). Children with HIV Infection: Collaborative Responsibilities of the Child Welfare and Medical Communities. *Social Work* 33(November-December):504-509.

Boland, M. G., Evans, P., Connor, E. M., & Oleske, J. M. (1988). Foster Care Needs of Children with HIV Infection. *AIDS and Public Policy Journal* 3(1):8-9.

Boneh, C. (1979). *Disruptions in Adoptive Placements: A Research Study*. Boston: Massachusetts Department of Public Welfare.

Bourguignon, F. P., & Watson, K. W. (1987). *After Adoption: A Manual for Professionals Working with Adoptive Families*. Springfield: Illinois Department of Children and Family Services.

Bourguignon, J. P., & Watson, K. (1989). *Toward Successful Adoption: A Study of Predictors in Special Needs Placements*. Springfield: Illinois Department of Children and Family Services.

Bowbly, J. (1951). Maternal Care and Mental Health. *World Health Organization Monograph No. 2*. Geneva: World Health Organization.

_____. (1969). *Attachment and Loss: Attachment*. New York: Basic Books.

_____. (1973). *Attachment and Loss: Separation, Anxiety and Anger*. New York: Basic Books.

_____. (1988). *A Secure Base: Clinical Applications of Attachment Theory*. London: Routledge (Tavistock Series).

Boyne, J., Denby, L., Kettenring, J. R., & Wheeler, W. (1984). *The Shadow of Success: A Statistical Analysis of Outcomes of Adoptions of Hard-to-Place Children*. Westfield, NJ: Spaulding for Children.

Brahal, R. M., Waterman, J., & Martin, H. P. (1981). The Social Cognitive Development of Abused Children. *Journal of Consulting and Clinical Psychology* 49:508-516.

Brodzinsky, D. (1987). Adjustment to Adoption: A Psychosocial Perspective. *Clinical Psychology Review* 7:25-47.

Busby, D. M., Glenn, E., Steggell, G. L., & Adamson, D. W. (1993). Treatment Issues for Survivors of Physical and Sexual Abuse. *Journal of Marital and Family Therapy* 19(4):377-392.

Cadoret, R. J., & Stewart, M. A. (1991). An Adoption Study of Attention Deficit/Hyperactivity/Aggression and Their Relationship to Adult Anti-social Personality. *Comprehensive Psychiatry* 32:73-82.

Caplan, G. (1974). *Support Systems and Community Mental Health: Lectures on Concept Development*. New York: Behavioral Publications.

Cardoret, R. J., Troughton, E., Bagford, J., & Woodworth, G. (1990). Genetic and Environmental Factors in Adoptee Antisocial Personality. *European Archives of Psychiatry and Neurological Sciences* 239:231-240.

Carter, B., & McGoldrick, M. (1988). Overview: The Changing Family Life Cycle-A Framework for Family Therapy. In B. Carter & M. McGoldrick, eds., *The Changing Family Life Cycle*, 2d ed. New York: Gardner Press, 3-28.

Cavaiola, A. A., & Schiff, M. (1988). Behavioral Sequelae of Physical and/or Sexual Abuse in Adolescents. *Child Abuse and Neglect* 12:181-188.

Ceccherini, V. (1991). Helping the Children of Romania. *Contemporary Review* 259(1511):281-284.

Centers for Disease Control. (1992). HIV/AIDS Surveillance Report. January:1-22, Atlanta, Georgia.

Cermack, S. A. (1994). Romanian Children Demonstrate Sensory Defensiveness. *Attachments* (spring):5-6.

Chasnoff, I. (1990). Maternal Drug Use. In *Crack and Other Addictions: Old Realities and New Challenges for Child Welfare*. Washington, DC: Child Welfare League of America, 10-20.

Chasnoff, I. F., Burns, K. A., Burns, W. J., & Schnoll, S. H. (1986). Prenatal Drug Exposure: Effects on Neonatal and Infant Growth and Development. *Journal of Neurobehavioral Toxicology and Teratology* 8(4): 357-362.

Chestang, L., & Heymann, I. (1976). Preparing Older Children for Adoption. *Public Welfare* 34(winter):335-340.

Child Welfare League of America. (1990). *Crack and Other Addictions: Old Realities and New Challenges for Child Welfare*. Washington, DC: Author.

Children Awaiting Parents. (1992). *Children in Foster Care Affected by HIV/AIDS*. New York: Author.

Christiansen, J. (1980). *Educational and Psychological Problems of Abused Children*. Saratoga, CA: Century 21.

Cicirelli, V. (1982). Sibling Influence throughout the Lifespan. In M. E. Lamb & B. Sutton-Smith, eds., *Sibling Relationships: Their Nature and Significance across the Life Span*. Hillsdale, NJ: Lawrence Erlbaum Associates, 267-284.

Clingempeel, W. G. (1981). Quasi-Kin Relationships and Marital Quality in Stepfather Families. *Journal of Personality and Social Psychology* 41:890-901.

Cochran, M. M., & Brassard, J. A. (1979). Child Development and Personal Social Networks. *Child Development* 50:601-616.

Cohen, E., Dinsmore, J., & Repella, J. (1989). Draft Working Paper on Drug Affected Babies, Alexandria, VA, American Prosecutors Research Institute.

Cohen, J. S. (1984). Adoption Breakdown with Older Children. In *Adoption: Current Issues and Trends*. Toronto: Butterworth.

Costin, L. B., Bell, C. J., & Downs, S. W. (1991). *Child Welfare: Policies and Practice*, 4th ed. New York: Longman.

Coyne, A., & Brown, M. E. (1985). Developmentally Disabled Children Can be Adopted. *Child Welfare* 64:607-615.

Crocker, A. C., Cohen, H. J., & Kastner, T. A. (1992). *HIV Infection and Developmental Disabilities: A Resource for Service Providers*. Baltimore: Paul H. Brookes.

Dahl, A. S., Cowgill, K. M., & Asumndsson, R. (1987). Life in Remarriage Families. *Social Work* 32(1):40-44.

Daro, D. (1988). *Confronting Child Abuse*. New York: Free Press.

DeFries, J. C., Plomin, R., Vandenberg, S. G., & Kuse, A. R. (1981). Parent-Offspring Resemblance for Cognitive Abilities in the Colorado Adoption Project: Biological, Adoptive, and Control Parents and One-Year-Old Children. *Intelligence* 5:245-277.

Deiner, P. L., Wilson, N. J., & Unger, D. G. (1988). Motivation and Characteristics of Families Who Adopt Children with Special Needs: An Empirical Study. *Topics in Early Childhood Special Education* 8(2):15-29.

Dennis, W. (1973). *Children of the Creche*. New York: Appleton-Century-Crofts.

DePanfilis, D., & Salus, M. K. (1992). *A Coordinated Response to Child Abuse and Neglect: A Basic Manual*. Washington, DC: US Department of Health and Human Services, Administration for Children and Families, National Center on Child Abuse and Neglect.

DiGiulio, J. F. (1987). Assuming the Adoptive Parent Role. *Social Casework: The Journal of Contemporary Social Work* November: 561-566.

Donley, K. S. (1990). Understanding Survival Behaviors: System Children in Adoption. Presentation sponsored by Four Oaks, Inc., Cedar Rapids, IA, September 6-7.

Dunn, J. (1983). Sibling Relationships in Early Childhood. *Child Development* 54(4):787-811.

————. (1985). *Sisters and Brothers*. Cambridge: Harvard University Press.

Elbow, M. (1986). From Caregiving to Parenting: Family Formation with Adopted Older Children. *Social Work* (September-October): 366-370.

Elmer, E. A. (1977). A Follow-up Study of Traumatized Children. *Pediatrics* 59:273-379.

Elonen, A. S., & Schwartz, E. M. (1969). A Longitudinal Study of Emotional, Social, and Academic Functioning of Adopted Children. *Child Welfare*, 47(2):72-78.

Emery, L. J., Anderson, G. R., & Annin, J. B. (1992). Child Welfare Concerns. In A. C. Crocker, J. J. Cohen, & T. A. Kastner, eds., *HIV Infection and Developmental Disabilities: A Resource for Service Providers*. Baltimore: Paul H. Brookes, 95-104.

Erickson, M. F., Egeland, B., & Pianta, R. (1989). The Effects of Maltreatment on the Development of Young Children. In D. Cicchetti & V. Carlson, eds., *Child Maltreatment: Theory and Research on the Causes and Consequences of Child Abuse and Neglect*, New York: Cambridge University Press, 647-684.

Falicov, C. J. (1988). Family Sociology and Family Therapy Contributions to the Family Development Framework: A Comparative Analysis and Thoughts on Future Trends. In C. J. Falicov, ed., *Family Transitions: Continuity and Change over the Life Cycle*. New York: Guilford Press, 3-54.

Fanshel, D. (1962). Approaches to Measuring Adjustment in Adoptive Parents. *Quantitative Approaches to Parent Selection*. New York: Child Welfare League of America.

Feigelman, W., & Silverman, A. R. (1983). *Chosen Children: New Patterns of Adoptive Relationships*. New York: Praeger.

Festinger, T. (1986). *Necessary Risk*. Washington, D C: Child Welfare League of America.

Finch, S., Fanshel, D., & Grundy, J. (1986). Factors Associated with the Discharge of Children from Foster Care. *Social Work Research and Abstracts* 22(1):10-18.

Finkelhor, D., & Browne, A. (1985). The Traumatic Impact of Child Sexual Abuse: A Conceptualization. *American Journal of Orthopsychiatry* 55:530-541.

_____. (1986). Initial and Long-term Effects: A Conceptual Framework. In D. Finkelhor (Ed.), *A Sourcebook on Child Sexual Abuse* (pp. 180-198. Beverly Hills, CA: Sage Publications.

Focus (1990). Newsletter from the National Council on Disability, Spring.

Franz, K. (1993). Final Report for the Post Adoption Family Support Project. Prepared for Northeast Ohio Adoption Services, Warren, Ohio, for the Department of Health and Human Services, Adoption Opportunities, Washington, D. C.

Freud, A., & Burlinghan, D. (1973). *Infants without Families: Reports on the Hamstead Nurseries 1939-1945*. New York: International Universities Press.

Froland, V. (1979). Talking about Networks That Help. In C. Froland & D. L. Pancoast, eds., *Networks for Helping*. Portland, OR: Portland State University, Regional Research Institute.

Garbarino, J. (1983). Social Support Networks: Rx for the Helping Professions. In J. K. Whittaker & J. Garbarino, eds., *Social Support Networks: Informal Helping in the Human Services*. New York: Aldine de Gruyter, 3-28.

General Accounting Office. (1990). Drug-Exposed Infants: A Generation at Risk. (GAO/HRD-90-138) Washington, DC: Human Resources Division.

George, C., & Main, M. (1979). Social Interactions of Young Abused Children: Approach, Avoidance and Aggression. *Child Development* 50:306-318.

Gil, M. (1978). Adoption of Older Children: The Problems Faced. *Social Casework* 59:272-278.

Giovannoni, J. M. (1985). Child Abuse and Neglect: An Overview. In J. Laird & A. Hartman, eds., *A Handbook of Child Welfare*. New York: Free Press, 193-212.

Girden, E. R. (1992). *ANOVA: Repeated Measures*. Newbury Park: Sage.

Glass, G. V., & Stanley, J. C. (1970). *Statistical Methods in Education and Psychology*. Englewood Cliffs, NJ: Prentice-Hall.

Gomly, D. S., & Shiono, P. H. (1991). Estimating the Number of Substance Exposed Children. *The Future of Children* 1(1), 17-25.

Gore, S. (1981). Stress-Buffering Functions of Social Support: An Appraisal and Clarification of Research Models. In B. S. Dohrenwend & B. P. Dohrenwend, eds., *Stressful Life Events and Their Contexts*. New York: Wiley, 202 222.

Gottlieb, B. (1988). Marshalling Social Support: The State of the Art in Research and Practice. In B. H. Gottlieb, ed., *Marshalling Social Support: Format, Processes and Effects.* San Francisco, CA: Sage, 11-51.

Green, A. (1978). The Psychopathology of Abused Children. *Journal of the American Academy of Child Psychology* 17:92-104.

Groze, V. (1986). Special Needs Adoption. *Children and Youth Services Review* 8:81-91.

———. (1990). *Subsidized Adoption in Iowa: A Study of Adoptive Families and Special Needs Children. Part I: The Family's Response. Part II: The Child's Response.* Des Moines, IA: Department of Human Services.

———. (1992). Adoption, Attachment and Self-Concept. *Child and Adolescent Social Work Journal* 9(2):169-191.

———. (1994). Clinical and Nonclinical Adoptive Families of Special Needs Children. *Families in Society* 75(2):90-104.

———. (in press). A 1 and 2 Year Follow-up Study of Adoptive Families and Special Needs Children. *Children and Youth Services Review.*

Groze, V., & Gruenewald, A. (1991). PARTNERS: A Model Program for Special Needs Adoptive Families in Stress. *Child Welfare* 70(5):581-589.

Groze, V., Haines-Simeon, M., & Barth, R. P. (1994). Barriers in Permanency Planning for Medically Fragile Children: Drug Affected Children and HIV Infected Children. *Child and Adolescent Social Work Journal* 11(1):63-85.

Groze, V., Haines-Simeon, M., & McMillen, J. C. (1992). Families Adopting Children with or At-Risk of HIV Infection: A Preliminary Study. *Child & Adolescent Social Work Journal* 9(5):409-426.

Groze, V., McMillen, J. C., & Haines-Simeon, M. (1993). Families Who Foster Children with HIV: A Maryland Pilot Study. *Child & Adolescent Social Work Journal* 10(1):67-87.

Groze, V., Persse, L., & Hill, L. (1993). *Social Support and the Adoptive Family.* Washington, DC: Department of Health and Human Services, Adoption Opportunities Program.

Groze, V., & Rosenberg, K. (forthcoming). *Treatment Issues of Adoptees Placed as Infants and as Older Children: Similarities and Differences.*

Groze, V., & Rosenthal, J. A. (1991a). A Structural Analysis of Families Adopting Children with Special Needs. *Families in Society* 72(8):469-481.

———. (1991b). Single Parents and Their Adopted Children: A Psychosocial Analysis. *Families in Society* 72 (2):67-77.

———. (1993). Attachment Theory and the Adoption of Children with Special Needs. *Social Work Research and Abstracts* 29(2):5-13.

Groze, V., Young, J., & Corcran-Rumppe, K. (1991). *Post Adoption Resources for Training, Networking and Evaluation Services (PARTNERS): Working with Special Needs Adoptive Families in Stress.* Washington, DC: Department of Health and Human Services, Adoption Opportunities.

Gurdin, P., & Anderson, G. R. (1987). Quality Care for Ill Children: AIDS-specialized Foster Family Homes. *Child Welfare* 66(4):291-302.

Gwinn, M., Pappaioanou, M., & George, J. R. (1991). Prevalence of HIV Infection in Childbearing Women in the United States: Surveillance Using Newborn Blood Samples. *The Journal of the American Medical Association* 265:1704-08.

Harper, J. (1991). Children's Play: The Differential Effects of Intrafamilial Physical and Sexual Abuse. *Child Abuse and Neglect* 15:89-98.

Hartman, A. (1984). *Working with Adoptive Families beyond Placement*. New York: Child Welfare League.

Hartman, A., & Laird, J. (1983). *Family-Centered Social Work Practice*. New York: Free Press.

Haupt, A. (1987). How Romania Tries to Govern Fertility. *Population Today* 15(2):3-4.

Hegar, R. L. (1988). Sibling Relations and Separations: Implications for Child Placement. *Social Service Review* 62:446-467.

_____ . (1993). Assessing Attachment, Permanence, and Kinship in Choosing Permanent Homes. *Child Welfare* 72(4):367-378.

Hines, J. R., Kessler, S., & Landers, C. (1991). *Children in Institutions in Central and Eastern Europe and a First Look at Alternative Approaches*. Florence, Italy: UNICEF International Child Development Centre.

Hirschi, T. (1969). *Causes of Delinquency*. Berkeley: University of California Press.

Hoffman-Plotkin, D., & Twentyman, C. (1984). A Multimodal Assessment of Behavior and Cognitive Deficits in Abused and Neglected Preschoolers. *Child Development* 55:794-802.

Hoopes, J. L. (1982). *Prediction in Child Development: A Longitudinal Study of Adoptive and Nonadoptive Families*. New York: Child Welfare League of America.

Hopkins, K. M. (1989). Emerging Patterns of Services and Case Finding for Children with HIV Infection. *Mental Retardation* 27(4):219-222.

House, J. (1981). *Work, Stress and Social Support*. Reading, MA:Addison-Wesley.

Hutchings, J. J. (1988). Pediatric AIDS: An Overview. *Children Today* 17(May-June):4-7.

Johnson, A. K., Edwards, R. L., & Puwak, H. C. (1993). Foster Care and Adoption Policy in Romania: Suggestions for International Intervention. *Child Welfare* 72, 5(September-October):489-506.

Johnson, A., & Groze, V. (1993). The Orphaned and Institutionalized Children of Romania. *Journal of Emotional and Behavioral Problems* 2(4):49-52.

Johnson, D., & Fein, E. (1991). The Concept of Attachment: Applications to Adoption. *Children and Youth Services Review* 13(5-6):397-412.

Johnson, D., Miller, L. C., Iverson, S., Thomas, W. Franchino, B., Dole, K., Kiernan, M. T., Georgieff, M. K., & Hostetter, M. K. (1992). The Health of Children Adopted from Romania. *Journal of the American Medical Association* 268(24):3446-3451.

Johnson, J. P., Prasanna, N., Hines, S. E., Seiden, S. W., Alger, L., Revie, D. R., O'Neil, K. M., & Heberl, R. (1989). Natural History and Serologic Diagnosis of Infants Born to Human Immunodeficiency Virus-Infected Women. *American Journal of Diseases of Children* 143(October):1147-1153.

Jones, M., & Niblett, R. (1985). To Split or Not to Split: The Placement of Siblings. *Adoption and Fostering* 9(2):26-29.

Kadushin, A. (1967). Reversibility of Trauma: A Follow-up Study of Children Adopted When Older. *Social Work* 12:22-33.

Kadushin, A., & Seidl, F. W. (1971). Adoption Failure: A Social Work Postmortem. *Social Work* 16(3):32-38.

Kagan, R. M., & Reid, W. J. (1986). Critical Factors in the Adoption of Emotionally Disturbed Youth. *Child Welfare* 65:63-74.

Kaler, S. R., & Freeman, B. J. (1994). An Analysis of Environmental Deprivation: Cognitive and Social Development in Romanian Orphans. *Journal of Child Psychology and Psychiatry and Allied Disciplines* 35(4):769-81.

Karoloff, N., & Friesen, B. (1991). Support Groups for Parents of Children with Emotional Disorders: A Comparison of Members and Non-members. *Community Mental Health Journal* 27(4):265-279.

Katz, L. (1986). Parental Stress and Factors for Success in Older-Child Adoption. *Child Welfare* 65(6):569-578.

Kaufman, J. and Cicchetti, D. (1989). Effects of maltreatment on school-age children's cocci emotional development: Assessments in a day camp setting. *Developmental Psychology*, 25(4):516-524.

Kaverola, C., Pound, J., Heger, A., & Lytle, C. (1993). Relationship of Child Sexual Abuse to Depression. *Child Abuse and Neglect* 17:393-400.

Kaye, K., Elkind, L., Goldberg, D., & Tytun, A. (1989). Birth outcomes of infants of Drug Abusing Mothers. *New York State Journal of Medicine* 89(5):256-261.

Kinard, E. M. (1980). Emotional Development in Physically Abused Children. *American Journal of Orthopsychiatry* 8:35-45.

Kirgan, D., Goodfield, G., & Campana, E. (1982). Attachment Impairment. San Rafael, CA: Mimeographed.

Kirk, D. H. (1984). *Shared Fate: A Theory and Method of Adoptive Relationships*, 2d ed. Port Angeles, WA: Ben-Simeon.

Klecka, W. R. (1980). *Discriminant Analysis*. New York: Sage.

Kline, D. F. (1977). Educational and Psychological Problems of Abused Children. *Child Abuse and Neglect* 1:301-307.

Kupecky, R. M. (1993). *Regina's Bag of Tricks*. Workshop presented at the 18th North American Conference on Adoptable Children, Milwaukee, WI, July 29-August 1.

LaBuda, M. C., DeFries, J. C., Plomin, R., & Fulker, D. W. (1986). Longitudinal Stability of Cognitive Ability from Infancy to Early Childhood: Genetic and Environmental Etiologies. *Child Development* 57:1142-1150.

Lamb, M., & Sutton-Smith, B., eds. (1982). *Sibling Relationships: Their Nature and Significance across the Life Span*. Hillsdale, NJ: Lawrence Erlbaum Associates.

Leeds, S. (1992). *Medical and Developmental Profiles of 148 Children Born HIV-Positive and Placed in Foster Families*. New York: Leake and Watts Services.

LePere, D. W., Davis, L. E., Couve, J., & McDonald, M. (1986). *Large Sibling Groups: Adoption Experiences*. Washington, DC: Child Welfare League of America.

Lie, G., & McMurtry, S. L. (1991). Foster Care for Sexually Abused Children: A Comparative Study. *Child Abuse and Neglect* 15:111-121.

Lipman, E. L., Offord, D. R., Boyle, M. H., & Racine, Y. A. (1993). Follow-up of Psychiatric and Educational Morbidity among Adopted Children. *Journal of the American Academy of Child and Adolescent Psychiatry*, 32(5):1007-1012.

Lipman, E. L., Offord, D. R., Racine, Y. A., & Boyle, M. H. (1992). Psychiatric Disorders in Adopted Children: A Profile from The Ontario Child Health Study. *Canadian Journal of Psychiatry* 37:627-633.

Little, R. E., Anderson, K. W., Ervin, C. H., & Worthington-Roberts, B. (1989). Maternal Alcohol Use during Breast-feeding and Infant Mental and Motor Development at One Year. *New England Journal of Medicine* 321(7):425-430.

Loehlin, J. C., Willerman, L., & Horn, J. M. (1982). Personality Resemblances between Unwed Mothers and Their Adopted-Away Offspring. *Journal of Personality and Social Psychology* 42(6):1089-1099.

_____ . (1985). Personality Resemblances in Adoptive Families When the Children Are Late Adolescent or Adult. *Journal of Personality and Social Psychology* 48(2):376-392.

_____ . (1987). Personality Resemblance in Adoptive Families: A 10-Year Follow-up. *Journal of Personality and Social Psychology* 53(5):961-969.

Louv, R. (1993). Why Parents Need One Another. *Parents Magazine*, July, 171-178.

Mackay, C., Cox, T., Burrows, G. I., & Lazzerini, T. (1978). An Inventory for the Measurement of Self-reported Stress and Arousal. *British Journal of Social and Clinical Psychology* 17:283-284.

Maguire, L. (1991). *Social Support Systems in Practice.* Silver Springs, MD: National Association of Social Workers Press.

Magura, S., Moses, B. S., & Jones, M. A. (1987). *Assessing Risk and Measuring Change in Families: The Family Risk Scales.* Washington, DC: Child Welfare League of America.

Main, M., Kaplan, N., & Cassidy, J. (1985). Security in Infancy, Childhood, and Adulthood: A Move to the Level of Representation. In I. Bretherton & E. Waters, eds., *Growing Points of Attachment Theory and Research. Monographs of the Society for Research in Child Development* 50(1-2, Serial No. 209): 66-104.

Main, M., & Weston, D. (1981). The Quality of the Toddler's Relationship to Mother and to Father: Related to Conflict Behavior and the Readiness to Establish New Relationships. *Child Development* 52:932-940.

Markese, R., & Soule, P. (1992). *Children in Foster Care Affected by HIV/AIDS: A Study of Laws and Policies regarding Testing, Confidentiality, Subsidy, Post-placement Services, and Recruitment of Foster and Adoptive Families.* Rochester, NY: Children Awaiting Parents.

McCubbin, H. I., & Patterson, J. M. (1982). Family Adaptation and Crisis. In H. I. McCubbin, A. E. Cauble, & J. M. Patterson, eds., *Family Stress, Coping, and Social Support* Springfield, IL: Charles C. Thomas, 26-47.

McGoldrick, M., & Carter, B. (1988). Forming a Remarried Family. In B. Carter & M. McGoldrick, eds., *The Changing Family Life Cycle*, 2d ed. New York: Gardner Press, 399-429.

McKenzie, J. K. (1993). Adoption of Children with Special Needs. In I. Schulman, ed., *The Future of Children.* Los Altos, CA: Center for the Future of Children, 62-76.

McMillen, J. C., & Groze, V. (1994). Using Placement Genograms in Child Welfare Practice. *Child Welfare* 72(4):307-318.

McMullan, S. J., Ames, E. W., & Chisholm, K. (submitted). The Development of Children Adopted from Romanian Orphanages.

McMullan, S. J., & Fisher, L. (1992). Developmental Progress of Romanian Orphanage Children in Canada. *Canadian Psychology* 33(2):504.

McMurtry, S. L., & Lie, G. W. (1992). Differential Exit Rates of Minority Children in Foster Care. *Social Work Research and Abstracts* 28(1):42-48.

McNamara, J., & McNamara, B. H. (1990). *Adoption and the Sexually Abused Child.* New York: Human Services Development Institute.

Meezan, W. & Shireman, J. (1982). Foster Parent Adoption: A Literature Review. *Child Welfare*, LXI (8):525-533.

Melina, L. R. (1986). *Raising Adopted Children.* New York: Harper & Row.

Moeller, T. P., Bachmann, G. A., & Moeller, J. R. (1993). The Combined Effects of Physical, Sexual, and Emotional Abuse during Childhood: Long-Term Health Consequences for Women. *Child Abuse and Neglect* 17:623-640.

Moorman, J. E., & Hernandez, D. J. (1989). Married-Couple Families with Step, Adopted, and Biological Children. *Demography* 26(2):267-277.

National Center on Child Abuse and Neglect (NCCAN). (1993). *National Child Abuse and Neglect Data System, Working Paper 2.* Gaithersburg, MD: Author.

Nelson, K. A. (1985). *On the Frontier of Adoption: A Study of Special-Needs Adoptive Families.* New York: Child Welfare League of America.

Novick, B. E. (1989). Pediatric AIDS: A Medical Overview. In J. M. Seibert & R. A. Olson, eds., *Children, Adolescents, and AIDS.* Lincoln: University of Nebraska Press, 1-23.

Oates, R., Forrest, D., & Peacock, A. (1985). Self-esteem of Abused Children. *Child Abuse and Neglect* 9:159-163.

Offord, D. R., Boyle, M. H., Racine, Y. A., Fleming, J. E., Cadman, D. T., Blum, H. M., Byrne, C., Links, P. S., Lipman, E. L., MacMillan, H. L., Grant, N.I.R., Sanford, M. N., Szatmari, P., Thomas, H., & Woodward, C. A. (1992). Outcome, Prognosis and Risk in a Longitudinal Follow-up Study. *Journal of the American Academy of Child and Adolescent Psychiatry* 31:916-923.

Oleske, J. (1987). Natural History of HIV Infection II. In B. K. Silverman & A. Waddell eds., *Report of the Surgeon General's Workshop on Children with HIV Infection and Their Families.* (DHHS Publication No. HRS-D-MS87-1). Washington, DC: U.S. Government Printing Office, 24-25.

Olson, D. H. (1989). Circumplex Model of Family Systems VIII: Family Assessment and Intervention. In D. H. Olson, C. S. Russell, & D. H. Sprenkle, eds., *Circumplex Model: Systemic Assessment and Treatment of Families.* New York: Haworth Press, 7-50.

Olson, D. H., Portner, J., & Lavee, Y. (1985). *FACES III.* St. Paul: Family Social Science, University of Minnesota.

Olson, D. H., Russell, C. S., & Sprenkle, D. H. (1979). Circumplex Model of Marital and Family Systems II: Empirical Studies and Clinical Intervention. In John Vincent, ed., *Advances in Family Intervention, Assessment and Theory.* Greenwich, CT: JAI Press, 128-176.

_____ . (1980). Marital and Family Therapy: A Decade Review. *Journal of Marriage and Family* 42:973-993.

_____ . (1983). Circumplex Model VI: Theoretical Update. *Family Process* 22:69-83.

Partridge S., Hornby, H., & McDonald, T. (1986). *Legacies of Loss, Visions of Gain: An Inside Look at Adoption Disruptions.* Portland: University of Southern Maine, Human Services Development Institute.

Patterson, J. M. (1988). Families Experiencing Stress. *Family Systems Medicine* 6(2):202-237.

Pearlin, L. I., & Schooler, C. (1982). The Structure of Coping. In H. I. McCubbin, A. E. Cauble, & J. M. Patterson, eds., *Family Stress, Coping, and Social Support.* Springfield, IL: Charles C. Thomas, 109-135.

Pearson, R. E. (1990). *Counseling and Social Support.* Newbury Park, CA: Sage.

Pfouts, J. H. (1976). The Sibling Relationship: A Forgotten Dimension. *Social Work* 21(3):200-203.

Phillips, M. (1990). Support Groups for Parents of Chronically Ill Children. *Pediatric Nursing* 16(4):404-406.

Piers, E. V. (1984). *Piers-Harris Children's Self-Concept Scale.* Los Angeles: WPS.

Piersma, H. L. (1987). Adopted Children and Inpatient Psychiatric Treatment: A Retrospective Study. *Psychiatric Hospital* 18:153-158.

Pilisuk, M., & Parks, S. H. (1983). Social Support and Family Stress. In H. I. McCubbin, M. B. Sussman, & J. M. Patterson, eds., *Social Stress and the Family: Advances in Developments in Family Stress Theory and Research.* New York: Haworth Press, 137-156.

Pinderhughes, E. E., & Rosenberg, K. (1990). Family Bonding with High Risk Placements: A Therapy Model That Promotes the Process of Becoming a Family. In L. M. Glidden, ed., *Formed Families: Adoption of Children with Handicaps.* New York: Haworth Press, 209-230.

Plomin, R., & DeFries, J. C. (1983). The Colorado Adoption Project. *Child Development* 54:276-289.

_____ . (1985). *Origins of Individual Differences in Infancy: The Colorado Adoption Project.* Orlando, FL: Academic Press.

_____ . (1985). A Parent-Offspring Adoption Study of Cognitive Abilities in Early Childhood. *Intelligence* 9:(4)-356.

Provence, S. A., & Lipton, R. C. (1962). *Infants in Institutions.* New York: International Universities Press.

Quinn, T. C. (1987). The Global Epidemiology of the Acquired Immunodeficiency Syndrome. In B. K. Silverman & A. Waddell, eds., *Report of the Surgeon General's Workshop on Children with HIV Infection and Their Families.* (DHHS Publication No. HRS-D-MS87-1). Washington, DC: U.S. Government Printing Office, 7-10.

Ramsey, P. W. (1992). Characteristics, Process, and Effectiveness of Community Support Groups: A Review of the Literature. *Family and Community Health* 15(3):38-48.

Ranieri, R. F., & Pratt, T. C. (1978). Sibling Therapy. *Social Work* 23:418-419.

Reid, W. J., Kagan, R. M., Kaminsky, A., & Helmer, K. (1987). Adoptions of Older Institutionalized Youth. *Social Casework* (March):140-149.

Reitz, M., & Watson, K. W. (1992). *Adoption and the Family System.* New York: The Guilford Press.

Roberts, M. (1984). Romanian Population Policy. *Population and Development Review* 10(3):570-573.

Rogeness, G. A., Hoppe, S. K., & Macedo, C. A. (1988). Psychopathology in Hospitalized Adopted Children. *Journal of the American Academy of Child and Adolescent Psychiatry* 27:628-631.

Rosenberg, E. B. (1992). *The Adoption Life Cycle: The Children and Their Families through the Years.* New York: Free Press.

Rosenthal, J. A., & Groze, V. (1990). Special Needs Adoption: A Study of Intact Families. *Social Service Review* 64(3):475-505.

_____ . (1991). Behavioral Problems of Special Needs Adopted Children. *Children and Youth Services Review* 13 (5-6):343-361.

_____ . (1992). *Special Needs Adoption: A Study of Intact Families.* New York: Praeger.

Rosenthal, J. A., Groze, V., & Aguilar, G. D. (1991). Adoption Outcomes for Children with Handicaps. *Child Welfare* 70(6):623-636.

Rosenthal, J. A., Groze, V., & Curiel, H. (1990). Race, Social Class and Special Needs Adoption. *Social Work* 35 November (6):532-539.

Rosenthal, J. A., Groze, V., Curiel, H., & Westcott, P. A. (1991). Transracial and Inracial Adoption of Special Needs Children. *Journal of Multicultural Social Work* 3(1):13-32.

Rosenthal, J. A., Schmidt, D., & Conner, J. (1988). Predictors of Special Needs Adoption Disruption: An Exploratory Study. *Children and Youth Services Review* 10:101-117.

Rothman, J. (1991). A Model of Case Management: Toward Empirically Based Practice. *Social Work* 36:520-528.

Rubinstein, A. (1987). Supportive Care and Treatment of Pediatric AIDS. In B. K. Silverman & A. Waddell, eds., *Report of the Surgeon General's Workshop on Children with HIV Infection and Their Families.* (DHHS Publication No. HRS-D-MS87-1). Washington, DC: U.S. Government Printing Office, 29-31.

_____. (1989). Background, Epidemiology, and Impact of HIV Infection in Children. *Mental Retardation*, (August):209-211.

Rutter , M. (1972). *Maternal Deprivation Reassessed.* London: C. Nicholas.

Sack, W. H., & Dale, D. (1982). Abuse and Deprivation in Failing Adoptions. *Child Abuse and Neglect* 6: 443-451.

Sandmaier, M. (1988). *When Love Is Not Enough.* Washington, DC: Child Welfare League of America.

Schaffer, J., & Lindstrom, C. Brief Solution-Focused Therapy with Adoptive Families (1990). In D. M. Brodzinsky & M. D. Schechter, eds., *The Psychology of Adoption.* New York: Oxford University Press, 253-272.

Schmidt, D. M. (1985). Presentation of Research Findings on Prevention of Adoption Disruption. In D. M. Schmidt, ed., *Proceedings of Conference on Special Needs Adoption: A Positive Perspective.* Denver: Colorado Department of Social Services, 7-10.

Schmidt, D. M., Rosenthal, J. A., & Bombeck, B. (1988). Parents' View of Adoption Disruption. *Children and Youth Services Review* 10:101-117.

Schneider, J., Griffith, D., & Chasnoff, I. J. (1989). Infants Exposed to Cocaine In Utero: Implications for Developmental Assessment and Intervention. *Infants and Young Children* (July): 25-36.

Schorr, E. L. (1987). Quoted in T. L. Shelton, E. S. Jeppson, & B. H. Johnson. *Family Centered Care for Children with Special Health Care Needs.* Washington, DC: Association for the Care of Children's Health, Division of Maternal and Child Health, U.S. Public Health Service.

Seglow, J., Pringle, M. K., & Wedge, P. (1972). *Growing Up Adopted.* Windsor, England: National Foundation for Education Research in England and Wales.

Select Committee on Children, Youth and Families. (1988). *A Generation in Jeopardy: Children and AIDS.* Washington DC: U.S. Government Printing Office.

Shireman, J., & Johnson, P. (1976). Single Persons as Adoptive Parents. *Social Service Review* 50:103-116.

_____. (1985). Single-Parent Adoptions: A Longitudinal Study. *Children and Youth Services Review* 7:321-334.

_____. (1986). A Longitudinal Study of Black Adoptions: Single Parent, Transracial, and Traditional. *Social Work* (May-June): 172-176.

Shireman, J. F. (1988). *Growing Up Adopted: An Examination of Some Major Issues.* Chicago: Chicago Child Care Society.

Showell, W., Hartley, R., & Allen, M. (1988). *Outcomes of Oregon's Family Therapy Program: A Descriptive Study of 999 Families.* Salem: Oregon State Children's Services Division.

Simon, R. J., & Altstein, H. (1977). *Transracial Adoption.* New York: Wiley.

————. (1981). *Transracial Adoption: A Follow-up.* Lexington, MA: Lexington Books.

————. (1987). *Transracial Adoptees and Their Families: A Study of Identity and Commitment.* New York: Praeger.

Simon, R. J., Altstein, H., & Melli, M. S. (1994). *The Case for Transracial Adoption.* Washington, DC: American University Press.

Simonds, R. J., & Rogers, M. F. (1992). Epidemiology of HIV in Children and Other Populations. In A. C. Crocker, H. J. Cohen, & T. A. Kastner, eds., *HIV Infection and Developmental Disabilities: A Resource for Service Providers.* Baltimore: Paul H. Brookes.

Skeels, H. M. (1938). Mental Development of Children in Foster Homes. *Journal of Consulting Psychology* 2:33-43.

Skodak, M. (1939). Children in Foster Homes. *University of Iowa Studies in Child Welfare* 16(1):156.

Skodak, M., & Skeels, H. M. (1945). A Follow-up Study of Children in Adoptive Homes. *The Journal of Genetic Psychology* 66:21-58.

————. (1949). "A Final Follow-up Study of One Hundred Adopted Children." *The Journal of Genetic Psychology,* 75:85-125.

Smith, D. W., & Sherwen, L. N. (1983). *Mothers and Their Adopted Children: The Bonding Process.* New York: Tiresias Press.

Smith, H. W. (1975). *Strategies of Social Research: The Methodological Imagination.* Englewood Cliffs, NJ: Prentice-Hall.

Smith, R. I., Coles, C. D., Lancaters, J., & Fernhoff, P. N. (1986). The Effect of Volume and Duration of Prenatal Ethanol Exposure on Neonatal Physical and Behavioral Development. *Journal of Neurobehavioral, Toxicology and Teratology* 8(4): 375-381.

Smith, S. L., & Howard, J. A. (1991). A Comparative Study of Successful and Disrupted Adoptions. *Journal of Social Service Review* 65:248-265.

————. (1994). The Impact of Previous Sexual Abuse on Children's Adjustment in Adoptive Placement. *Social Work* 39(5):491-501.

Spitz, R. A. (1945). Hospitalism: An Inquiry into the Genesis of Psychiatric Conditions in Early Childhood. *Psychoanalytic Study of the Child* 1:53-74.

Staff, I., Fein, E., & Johnson, D. B. (1993). Methodological Issues in Studying Sibling Placement. *Social Work Research and Abstracts* 29(2):35-37.

Stewart, R., & Marvin, R. S. (1984). Sibling Relations: The Role of Conceptual Perspective-taking in the Ontogeny of Sibling Caregiving. *Child Development* 55(4):1322-1332.

Stolley, K. S. (1993). Statistics on Adoption in the United States. In I. Schulman, ed. *The Future of Children.* Los Altos, CA: Center for the Future of Children, 26-42.

Sutton-Smith, B. (1982). Birth Order and Sibling Status Effects. In M. E. Lamb & B. Sutton-Smith, eds., *Sibling Relationships: Their Nature and Significance across the Life Span.* Hillsdale, NJ: Lawrence Erlbaum Associates, 153-165.

Talen, M. R., & Lehr, M. L. (1984). A Structural and Developmental Analysis of Symptomatic Adopted Children and Their Families. *Journal of Marital and Family Therapy* 10(4):381-391.

Tatara, T. (1988). *Characteristics of Children in Substitute and Adoptive Care: A Statistical Summary of the VCIS National Child Welfare Data Base.* Washington, DC: The American Public Welfare Association.

_____ . (1993). *Characteristics of Children in Substitute and Adoptive Care: A Statistical Summary of the VCIS National Child Welfare Data Base.*Washington, DC: American Public Welfare Association.

Timberlake, E. M., & Hamlin, E. R. (1982). The Sibling Group: A Neglected Dimension of Placement. *Child Welfare* 61(8):545-552.

Tizard, B. (1977). *Adoption: A Second Chance.* New York: Free Press.

Tourse, P., & Gundersen, L. (1988). Adopting and Fostering Children with AIDS: Policies in Progress. *Children Today* 17(3)(May-June): 15-19.

Tracy, E. (1990). Identifying Social Support Resources of At-Risk Families. *Social Work* 35(3):252-258.

Tracy, E. M., & Whittaker, J. K. (1990). The Social Network Map: Assessing Social Support in Clinical Practice. *Families in Society* (October):461-470.

Unger, C., Dwarshuis, G., & Johnson, E. (1977). *Chaos, Madness and Unpredictability.... Placing the Child with Ears like Uncle Harry's.* Chelsea, MI: Spaulding for Children.

Unger, D. G., Deiner, P., & Wilson, N. (1988). Families Who Adopt Children with Special Needs. *Children and Youth Services Review* 10:317-328.

Urban Systems Research & Engineering. (1985). *Evaluation of State Activities with Regard to Adoption Disruption.* Washington, DC: Urban Research and Engineering.

U.S. Department of Health and Human Services (DHHS). (1988). *Study Findings: Study of National Incidence and Prevalence of Child Abuse and Neglect, 1988.* Washington, DC: Author.

Vondra, J. I., Barnett, D., & Cicchetti, D. (1990). Self-concept, Motivation, and Competence among Preschoolers from Maltreating and Comparison Families. *Child Abuse and Neglect* 14:525-540.

Wachsman, L., Schuetz, S., Chan, L. S., & Wingert, W. A. (1989). What happens to babies exposed to Phencyclidine (PCP) in Utero. *American Journal of Drug and Alcohol Abuse* 15(1): 31-39.

Walsh, J. A. (1991). *A Parent Survey: Assesssing Post Adoption Services.* Chicago: Illinois Department of Children and Family Services.

Ward, M. (1984). Sibling Ties in Foster Care and Adoption Planning. *Child Welfare* 63(4):321-332.

Waters, E., & Deane, K. E. (1985). Defining and Assessing Individual Differences in Attachment Relationships: Q-Methodology and the Organization of Behavior in Infancy and Early Childhood. In I. Bretherton & E. Waters, eds., *Growing Points of Attachment Theory and Research. Monographs of the Society for Research in Child Development* 50(1-2, Serial No. 209):41-65.

Webb, E. J., Campbell, D. T., Schwartz, R. D., & Sechrest, L. (1966). *Unobtrusive Measures: Nonreactive Research in the Social Sciences.* Chicago: Rand McNally.

Wedge, P., & Mantel, G. (1991). *Sibling Groups and Social Work.* Brookfield: Avebury Press.

Westhues, A., & Cohen, J. S. (1990). Preventing Disruption of Special-Needs Adoptions. *Child Welfare* 69(2):141-156.

Wheeler, C. (1978). *Where Am I Going? Making a Life Story Book.* Juneau, AK: Winking Owl Press.

Whittaker, J. K. (1983a). Mutual Helping in Human Service Practice. In J. K. Whittaker & J. Garbarino, eds., *Social Support Networks: Informal Helping in the Human Services*. New York: Aldine de Gruyter, 29-67.

————. (1983b). Social Support Networks in Child Welfare. In J. K. Whittaker and J. Garbarino (eds.), *Social Support Networks: Informal Helping in the Human Services*. New York: Aldine de Gruyter, 167-187.

Whittaker, J. K., & Garbarino, J. (1983). *Social Support Networks: Informal Helping in the Human Services*. New York: Aldine de Gruyter.

Winkler, R. C., Brown, D. W., van Keppel, M., & Blanchard, A. (1988). *Clinical Practice in Adoption*. New York: Pergamon Press.

Wodarski, J. S., Kurtz, P. D., Gaudin, J. M., & Howing, P. T. (1990). Maltreatment and the School-Age Child: Major Academic, Socioemotional, and Adaptive Outcomes. *Social Work* 35(6):506-513.

Woodruff, G., & Sterzin, E. D. (1988). The Transagency Approach: A Model for Serving Child with HIV Infection and Their Families. *Children Today* 3(May-June):9-14.

Yates, A. (1981). Narcissistic Traits in Certain Abused Children. *American Journal of Orthopsychiatry* 51:55-62.

Young, J., Corcran-Rumppe, K., & Groze, V. (1992). Integrating Special-Needs Adoption and Residential Treatment. *Child Welfare* 71(6):513-526.

Zuckerman, B. (1993). Developmental Considerations for Drug- and AIDS-Affected Infants. In R. Barth, J. Pietrzak, & M. Ramler, eds., *Families Living with Drugs and HIV*. New York: Guilford, 37-60

Zwimpfer, D. M. (1983). Indicators of Adoption Breakdown. *Social Casework: The Journal of Contemporary Social Work* 64:169-177.

Index

About the Author

VICTOR GROZE is Associate Dean of Academic Affairs and Associate Professor of the Mandel School of Applied Social Sciences at Case Western Reserve University. He is the co-author of *Special-Needs Adoption: A Study of Intact Families* (Praeger, 1992).

ISBN 0-275-95343-2

90000>

9 780275 953430

EAN

HARDCOVER BAR CODE